Russian Literature: A Very Short Introduction

'a great pleasure to read. It is a sophisticated, erudite, searching, and subtle piece of work. It is written in a lively and stimulating manner, and displays a range to which few of Dr Kelly's peers in the field of Russian scholarship can aspire.'
Phil Cavendish, School of Slavonic and East European Studies, University of London

'a brilliant essay, written with elegance, informed, incisive, provocative . . . you may love it, perhaps loathe it, or feel perplexed, but not remain indifferent.'
A. G. Cross, Cambridge University

'Kelly's brief but clear and effective study [is] a skilful blending of literary personalities rather than leaning simply on chronology . . . it is an original book, well done and documented, and extremely readable.'
John Bayley, St Catherine's College, Oxford University

Very Short Introductions available now:

For more information visit our web site:
www.oup.co.uk/general/vsi/

Catriona Kelly

RUSSIAN
LITERATURE

A Very Short Introduction

OXFORD
UNIVERSITY PRESS

OXFORD
UNIVERSITY PRESS

Great Clarendon Street, Oxford OX2 6DP

Oxford University Press is a department of the University of Oxford.
It furthers the University's objective of excellence in research, scholarship,
and education by publishing worldwide in

Oxford New York

Auckland Bangkok Buenos Aires Cape Town Chennai
Dar es Salaam Delhi Hong Kong Istanbul Karachi Kolkata
Kuala Lumpur Madrid Melbourne Mexico City Mumbai Nairobi
São Paulo Shanghai Taipei Tokyo Toronto

Oxford is a registered trade mark of Oxford University Press
in the UK and in certain other countries

Published in the United States
by Oxford University Press Inc., New York

British Library Cataloguing in Publication Data
Data available

ISBN 978-0-19-280144-9

9 10

Typeset by RefineCatch Ltd., Bungay, Suffolk
Printed in Great Britain by
Ashford Colour Press Ltd, Gosport, Hants.

Preface

Introductions to Russian literature, like introductions to national literatures more generally, traditionally take three forms. One type is an outine of what is known as the 'canon', the lives and works of famous writers – Pushkin, Dostoevsky, Tolstoy, Turgenev, Chekhov, with a supporting cast of lesser figures from the nineteenth century, and of major ones from the twentieth. A second type is a sketch of literary movements and cultural institutions: Neo-Classicism, Romanticism, Realism, Symbolism, Modernism, Socialist Realism; censorship, the Soviet Writers' Union, and literary dissidence. A third way of approaching the exercise, one preferred by writers as opposed to academics, is personal appreciation. In, say, Vladimir Nabokov's *Lectures on Russian Literature*, or Joseph Brodsky's *Less than One*, the selection of material is explicitly subjective, and vehement advocacy of some writers sits alongside equally energetic debunking of others.

There are also less obvious ways of writing introductions. One is the survey organized round a strong central thesis. Yury Tynyanov's brilliant book *Archaists and Innovators* (1929), for instance, argued that literary evolution developed out of writers' attitudes towards existing texts, whose ways of representing the world might be inertly copied, actively rejected, or at once absorbed and transformed. Another is the in-depth analysis of some technical aspect of the literary language. Mikhail Gasparov's history of Russian versification, for example, examines how preferences for metrical forms have changed over the course of time and scrutinizes the weight of meaning carried by particular metrical measures at a given point in history.

This book does not fall into any of these categories, least of all the first two. There are many excellent linear outlines of Russian literary history already: there is no place for another one, particularly not one that would need to simplify beyond recognition a literary culture with a large number of important writers, many of whom wrote big, complex books. Equally, I am wary of settling on some central 'big idea', given that there are already far too many ruminations on Russian literature that reduce sophisticated texts to inane clichés: the 'superfluous man' as the central theme of fiction, and so on. On the other hand, a theoretical discussion such as Tynyanov's needs room to breathe, and is hard to follow if the source material it attempts to explain is unfamiliar. So what I have decided to do is to follow the lead of an earlier Very Short Introduction, Mary Beard and John Henderson's eloquent and captivating *Classics*. Rather than running through the Peloponnesian Wars, Greeks and Persians, Athens as the birthplace of democracy, Rome as the birthplace of plumbing, the Conquest of Britain, and other landmarks of the subject as it used to be taught in the school room, *Classics* focuses on one particular artefact, the friezes from the Temple of Apollo at Bassae in Arcadia, using them as the starting point of a wide-ranging exploration of issues that are of current concern in the professional study of the Ancient World and of changing attitudes to the classical past.

A comparable way of organizing an introduction, both to Russian literature and to the ways of thinking and arguing about it, is to centre it on the Russian equivalent of Shakespeare, if not of the Bassae Marbles, Aleksandr Pushkin (1799–1837). Pushkin's writings themselves touch on many central themes in contemporary literary history, from the colonization of the Caucasus to salon culture. Many different critical approaches have been applied to them, from textology, or the comparison of manuscript variants, to Formalism, to feminism. The development of the 'Pushkin myth' (the writer as 'the founding father of Russian literature') raises all kinds of interesting questions about how literary history is made, about how the idea of a 'national literature' comes into being, and about the way in which these processes made certain kinds of writing seem marginal (writing by Russian women, for instance).

Approaching a national literature in this way does not mean exposing an act of deception perpetrated on readers by patriotic critics. Pushkin – like Dante, Shakespeare, or Goethe – was gifted with outstanding talent and intellectual depth: his writing is profoundly rewarding. But the reputations of such national writers can be intimidating, surrounded as they are by critical guard-dogs, who (as is only to be expected of guard-dogs) often seem less concerned to celebrate what they are protecting than to keep others away from it. Reputations of this kind sometimes generate rather lazy reactions on the part of critics, too. (Consider the phrase I used a couple of sentences earlier, 'profoundly rewarding': what does this actually mean?) Pushkin and other great Russian writers should not be seen as members of some artistic Politburo, receiving what Soviet meetings used to describe as 'stormy applause turning into an ovation' from a captive audience of contemporaries and later generations. They were often at loggerheads with each other and with the Russian public, while the efforts of successive regimes to press dead writers into service as prophets of official ideologies stood in stark contrast to the intolerance of the same regimes for living writers who would not keep their mouths shut (or their pens at rest). There is quite a lot in this book that is controversial, too, but it is meant to be provocative in an active sense – to stimulate reflection and debate. You will not finish it knowing everything there is to know about Russian literature, but you might, I hope, be inspired to find out more about one of the world's great literary cultures and to share my enthusiasm for thinking and writing about it.

Although this book is not meant to be a conventional literary history, I am determined to follow convention in one respect: by thanking those who helped with the writing of it. George Miller gently bullied me into the idea of writing a 'very short' introduction in the first place, and offered an exemplary mixture of commitment, constructive criticism, and technical guidance as the book took shape. Catherine Humphries and Alyson Lacewing saw the typescript through to press. Several anonymous readers made suggestions that helped me improve the first draft; more general help with lines of approach came from conversations with friends such as Mikhail Leonovich Gasparov, Barbara Heldt, Stephen Lovell, David Shepherd, Gerry Smith, and Alexander Zholkovsky, as well as from the studies of Russian literature and culture listed in my suggestions for further reading. Martin McLaughlin's gift of his Calvino translation was a great help with Chapter 1.

In an introductory book of this kind, though, it is above all one's teachers that one thinks of. In my undergraduate days at Oxford, Anne Pennington's wise tolerance and deep love of Russian poetry was complemented by Ronald Hingley's fierce expression of enthusiasms and detestations, and insistence that Russian writers must be seen as part of a wider literary world. I hope this book is a worthy tribute to them, and also to the students I have taught in Oxford and at the University of London, whose sceptical questions, creative ideas, and refusal to take anything for granted are a constant delight and an unfailing inspiration.

Contents

List of illustrations

List of Maps

Map 1 The Russian Empire, showing places with literary associations.

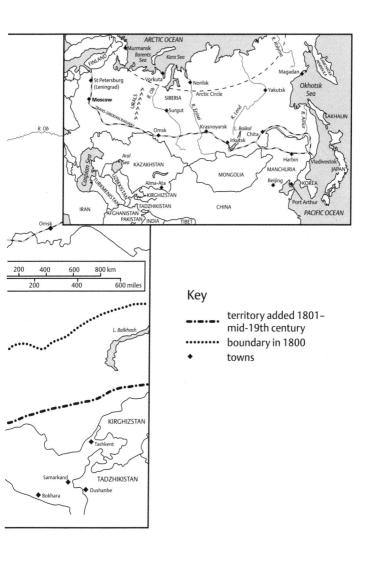

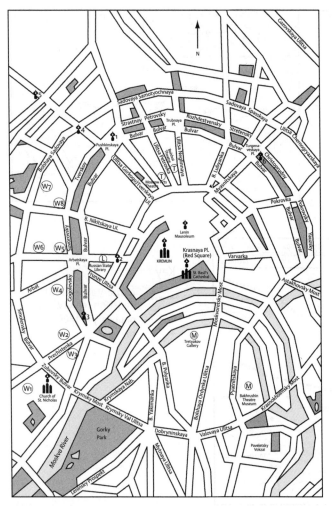

Map 2 Central Moscow, showing some of the main monuments and museums.

Key

- Ⓜ Museums
- Ⓣ Theatres
- Ⓛ Libraries
- 🛐 Churches

Ⓦ Writer's museums

- Ⓦ1 L. Tolstoy museum ('Tolstoy house')
- Ⓦ2 Pushkin museum
- Ⓦ3 L. Tolstoy museum
- Ⓦ4 Hertsen (memorial house)
- Ⓦ5 Gogol
- Ⓦ6 Tsvetaeva (memorial apartment)
- Ⓦ7 Chekhov (memorial house)
- Ⓦ8 Gorky

🛉 Monuments

- 🛉1 Pushkin (1880)
- 🛉2 Dostoevsky (1981)
- 🛉3 Gogol (1909/1952)
- 🛉4 Mayakovsky (1958)
- 🛉5 Gorky (1951)
- 🛉6 Bulgakov (1991)

Chapter 1
Testament

Which of us can understand Pushkin? We knew Pushkin only in translation [. . .] and we liked his short stories much less than Nathaniel Hawthorne's; and obviously, we were wrong, for because of limitations of language we were debarred from seeing something that is as obvious to unsealed eyes as the difference between a mule and a Derby winner.

(Rebecca West, 1941)

In 1925, the Anglo-Russian literary critic D. S. Mirsky began *Modern Russian Literature*, a pioneering 'very short' introduction published by Oxford University Press, by referring to Pushkin.

It is indeed difficult for the foreigner, perhaps impossible if he is ignorant of the language, to believe in the supreme greatness of Pushkin among Russian writers. Yet it is necessary for him to accept the belief, even if he disagrees with it. Otherwise every idea he may form of Russian literature and Russian civilization will be inadequate and out of proportion with reality.

Seven decades later, Pushkin is still acknowledged as 'supremely great' among Russian writers by his compatriots, and this is still likely to strike foreign readers as odd. Outside its home, Russian literature is associated first and foremost with prose, and particularly with prose that is rich in

1. Portrait of Aleksandr Pushkin.

This 1827 portrait of Alexandr Pushkin (1799–1837) by Vasily Tropinin, done from life by an artist who was the favoured painter of Moscow's 'middling sort' (successful merchants, civil servants, and respectable writers) is at first sight a workaday likeness. In contrast to a contemporary, Orest Kiprensky, who produced a full-blown Romantic portrait of Pushkin, eyes raised, arms folded, and statue of the Muse at his back, Tropinin gives the poet only one 'writerly' accessory, the sheaf of manuscript under his right arm. At the same time, Pushkin is handled rather differently from Tropinin's other subjects. His fraying scarf, carelessly knotted at his badly ironed collar, and long dirty fingernails, suggest unconcern with trivialities such as grooming; his sideways gaze conveys abstraction; and his prominent strabismus (barely noticeable in most portraits) implies internal conflict. The picture shows Pushkin at the pinnacle of his lifetime fame. A byword for youthful brilliance even in an age where precocity was taken for granted (he had begun publishing while still at the Lyceum School in Tsarskoe Selo, and his early works included the sparkling mock-epic *Ruslan and Ludmilla*, written in his late teens), Pushkin achieved still greater notoriety when he was exiled for political insubordination in 1820. Outside the capital until 1826, he remained at the centre of literary life: *The Prisoner of the Caucasus* (1822), the early chapters of *Evgeny Onegin*, and the lyric poems of 1820–5 had a huge popular and literary success and remained the benchmark of his achievement for many critics and ordinary readers. During the late 1820s and early 1830s, Pushkin's circumstances were to become increasingly difficult, as a result of political surveillance, a troubled marriage, and a problematic relationship with his readers. Later works, such as the historical narrative poem *Poltava* (1828), received a relatively cool reception, and the last years of the poet's life, culminating in his death in a duel in January 1837, saw mounting personal and artistic isolation. But between 1826 and 1830, he produced a run of masterpieces: many of his greatest lyric poems, his first published experiments in prose, and several outstanding narrative poems, as well as the later chapters of *Evgeny Onegin*.

ideas and devotes itself to the exploration of moral dilemmas. Since the late nineteenth century, it has been Tolstoy and Dostoevsky, the authors of vast novels of exactly this kind, who have been acknowledged, among Western readers, as the greatest writers of Russia. Tolstoy's *War and Peace* (1865–9), which argues that human beings can exercise control over events only if they recognize their own powerlessness, yet breathes individuality into a vast range of characters, appears regularly in lists of the ten most important books of all time. The ethical concerns set out by Dostoevsky, above all the question of whether morality is possible in a world without God, anticipated some of the most important concerns of modern philosophy, from Nietzsche to Sartre.

Pushkin wrote no large novels, and he does not even seem particularly 'Russian' in other ways, not even as 'Russian' as Turgenev. Turgenev's *Fathers and Sons* (1862) has a main character, Bazarov, whose obsession with social utility (he insists that the dissecting of frogs is superior to water-colour painting) seems satisfactorily strange because it is so hyperbolic. And the novel's country estate setting is at once charming and exotic, with its serf mistress, its ribboned dogs, and its duel fought over an imagined matter of honour. It is easy to trace a line between *Fathers and Sons* and Chekhov's plays, but far less easy to see how *Evgeny Onegin* – with its wayward digressions, its urbane and ironic tone, and its curious air of repressed emotion – might be a forerunner of Tolstoy's *Anna Karenina* (1875–7) or of Dostoevsky's *The Idiot* (1868). The combination of wit with the melancholy appreciation that happiness may be most elusive when easiest to realize makes the book seem more like a successor to Jane Austen's *Persuasion*. To be sure, it has some impressive English-language descendants – they include Nabokov's *Lolita* and Vikram Seth's verse novel about San Francisco, *The Golden Gate* – but these arch and self-conscious texts simply enhance Western readers' conviction that Pushkin is peculiar in terms of his own, supposedly immediate and spontaneous, culture.

Yet all the major Russian writers were avid readers of European literature; if they reacted against it, they also learned from it. *Anna Karenina* may be at some level a riposte to *Madame Bovary*, but there is a direct connection between an image in the opening pages of Flaubert's novel – Charles Bovary's hideous hat standing for the inconsequential life remarked by the author alone – and the insignificant stubborn burdock that Tolstoy's narrator notices at the beginning of *Hadji Murat*. During the eighteenth century, Russians had been haunted by fears that their literature was too imitative, too dominated by translations. Such fears were replaced during the nineteenth century by pride in native achievements, but receptivity to French, English, German, Spanish, and Italian literature continued. Even writers who had only a poor knowledge of Western languages absorbed foreign material avidly. Dostoevsky's novels were as indebted to Dickens as they were to Gogol. Though the writer detested the real England when he visited in 1862, that only confirmed his adulation for Dickens. After 1917, love of foreign literature survived not only the bitterness of exile, but the cultural isolation endured by writers who stayed behind in the Soviet Union. Anna Akhmatova's admiration for T. S. Eliot and James Joyce, and Joseph Brodsky's for John Donne, are only two of the better-known relationships with Western literature; a more unexpected instance is Marina Tsvetaeva's enthusiasm for the best-selling American novelist Pearl S. Buck.

By no means all the commentators who shaped Anglophone readers' views of Russian literature were unaware of the artistic affinity of

'Russian' and 'Western' traditions. Many were authors themselves – indeed, the most impressive English-language interpretations of Russian literature have tended to be literary rather than critical. The short stories of Chekhov, in particular, left marks on the work of writers in English such as Katherine Mansfield, Elizabeth Bowen, Sean O'Faolain, Raymond Carver, Alice Munro, Richard Ford, and William Trevor. Chekhov's stories were models of how to contrive small-scale narratives that almost evaded the onward drive of plot, and captured a character's entire world in a few moments that were both exemplary and elusive. Chekhov's writing accorded well with Anglophone admiration for unnoticeable virtuosity (it is not for nothing that the term 'craft' also means 'stealth'). But if greatness in prose involves hardly seeming to write literature at all, then some of Pushkin's narratives – *The Prisoner of the Caucasus* (1822), *Dubrovsky* (1832–3), or *The Captain's Daughter* (1836) – are likely to disappoint. Here, plot matters a great deal, and the need to provide a resolute ending seems uppermost. In addition, Pushkin's closeness to French models (Chateaubriand's *René* or Constant's *Adolphe*, the poetry of Parny and Lamartine) does him no service in Anglophone culture, which has traditionally equated 'French' with 'trite, superficial, and pretentious'.

To be fair, Pushkin's strangeness is not something felt only by foreigners. Russian commentators have remarked it too. Those of pro-Western sympathies have considered it a sign of Pushkin's unique status as a truly civilized person in a society of shameful backwardness; for nationalists, on the other hand, it has been a signal tragedy, a symbol of the alienation of intellectuals from the 'Russian people'. The philosopher Gustav Shpet, a late follower of the nineteenth-century Slavophiles (the movement that arose in the 1830s in order to lament the harm that had been done to Russian culture by Westernization), saw Pushkin as 'an accident'. His writing was 'precisely his writing, the writing of a genius who did not emerge from the Russian national spirit'. But whatever their feelings about Pushkin's expression (or not) of the 'national spirit', Russians universally acknowledge him as a master of the language. It is worth pausing a moment to consider why.

All Pushkin's writings, from his warmly intimate and at times shockingly immediate letters, to his most considered, reserved, and formal lyric poems, particularly exemplify two characteristics that have a peculiar weight in Russian literary culture, even if they are by no means unique to that culture. The first is an intense sensitivity to stylistic register, to the connotations of words. This sensitivity homes in particularly on the opposition between words derived from Church Slavonic, the liturgical language of Russian Orthodoxy, and those of native Russian origin. *Zlatyi* and *zolotoi* are translatable only as 'golden', *mladyi* and *molodoi* only as 'young', yet the words are as different in terms of their associations as the English words 'leathern' and 'leather', 'burthern' and 'burden'. Pushkin's poetry is peculiarly sophisticated in its blending of these and other stylistic levels. It is also subtle in its exploitation of formal features – metre, assonance, and alliteration. An extraordinary level of stylistic density is offset by a level of compression that exploits to the full the resources offered by Russian grammar, which allows a good deal more ellipsis (the omission of words that a reader can be expected to supply by inference) than is ordinarily possible in English. Pushkin's poetry works both with and against the norms of literary Russian. It shares the adventurous playfulness of all good writing in the language, yet at the same time keeps a tight hold upon the rhetorical expansion that is natural to a literary tradition where creative repetition, the so-called 'weaving of words', is actively sought rather than avoided – as it tends to be avoided in mandarinic British or American usage, as opposed to Irish, African, or British or American vernacular, English. This sense of working *against* linguistic norms is one reason why the Russian critic and theorist Roman Jakobson asserted that modern readers wanting to understand Pushkin 'must wholly abandon ordinary aesthetic criteria'.

One could, then, say of Pushkin, as the playwright Sheridan did of Horace: 'To give the literal meaning, it should be in verse'. But metrical paraphrases of Pushkin are rather apt to sound like the work of some justly forgotten nineteenth-century poetaster:

> The woods have doff'd their garb of purply gold;
> The faded fields with silver frost are steaming;
> Through the pale clouds the sun, reluctant gleaming,
> Behind the circling hills his disk hath roll'd.

This version of the opening lines of '19 October 1825', translated by Thomas Budge Shaw, teacher of English at the Tsarskoe Selo Lyceum (the school Pushkin attended) in the 1840s, was highly regarded in its time. But now it sounds unbearably fusty. This is not Shaw's fault. He is strictly accurate in metrical terms; though inventing some 'pale clouds' and 'steaming frost', he closely follows the sense of the Russian too, which is quite an achievement. The problem is that linguistic taste has altered in the English-speaking world as it has not in Russia. Though Pushkin's style in this piece has a formality that recalls eighteenth-century elegies, the Russian words rendered by 'hath roll'd' or 'doff'd' are still standard in colloquial speech, not mothballed by centuries of non-use. 'Purply-gold' is a convincing rendition of the emotional and highly-coloured adjective *bagryanyi* (crimson: the word *bagryanitsa* is used for silk brocade in that colour), but it provokes dyspepsia in Anglophone readers of poetry who have swallowed (as many have) T. S. Eliot's strictures against high-style poeticisms. Given that the phrases that most move Russian readers are likely to strike English-speaking ones as particularly laughable or tasteless, it follows that translations admired by native speakers of Russian tend to go down badly with native speakers of English, and vice versa. Anglophone translators who followed Joseph Brodsky's advice, and rendered Mandelstam in the manner of late Yeats, would be unlikely to enjoy the warm esteem of their contemporaries. Even if Pushkin had (as with Rabelais and Urquhart) been translated by a brilliant contemporary, the translation would probably strike modern readers as disappointing. The reaction of Rebecca West, used as the chapter epigraph, typifies the frustration of those who have tried to read Pushkin in English and not been able to get the point.

But one should not get too melodramatic about this. Pious sentiments about the untranslatability of Pushkin seem to be a genre requirement in every introduction to the writer: they are as true, but also as false, as platitudes about poetry getting lost in translation. Certainly, Pushkin is best read in Russian, just as Aeschylus is in Greek, or Dante in Italian. But reading these writers in English is better than not reading them at all. And, as the cases of Shakespeare in Russian or Dostoevsky in English make clear, great writers are best served by a proliferation of translations. Only if the whole range of a writer's work is available does his or her diversity become clear. At least until the 1990s, when more ambitious translation projects got under way, Pushkin in English meant *Evgeny Onegin* plus a handful of famous love poems – 'I remember the wonderful moment' (1825), 'I loved you' (1829), 'On the hills of Georgia' (1829). He came across as a sort of Russian Byron, though much of his verse is far closer in spirit to Pope, or then again to Shelley, Blake, Wordsworth, or even Burns. The more translations there are, the more likely readers are to find in one or other poem, or in one or other version of the same poem, the 'sense of discovery' that is (as the Italian writer Italo Calvino has argued) one of the most important reasons for reading a classic writer.

This 'sense of discovery' does not necessarily make itself felt when the text reads easily in English. Ted Hughes's version of Pushkin's Romantic poem 'The Prophet' (1827) uses harsh consonant clashes not found in the original, as well as dispensing with rhyme. But the use of a rough, abrasive manner is probably the only way in which the mythic force of Pushkin's belief in the poet's messianic gifts (not a notion with which an Anglophone audience is immediately comfortable) could be captured in 1990s English. Nabokov's annotated prose version of *Evgeny Onegin*, a supplement to the Pushkin text rather than an autonomous 'translation' in the ordinary sense, shows another method of proceeding, one according to which the rendering is deliberately made so inadequate to the original as to leave the latter's integrity intact.

My own translation of Pushkin's 1836 poem 'I have raised myself a monument' below is of this second kind – finickingly literal, without pretensions to being an independent poem. It is nearly half as long again in terms of word count, an inevitable result of the fact that word-units are longer, on average, in Russian than in English. Therefore, the English sounds much more verbose than the Russian. While some alliteration survives (by pure chance), the metre, with the use of the shortened fourth line in each stanza to puncture the grandeur of the first three, does not. There are some problems with vocabulary too. The beautiful word *podlunnyi* becomes sublunar, a word that sounds like a citation from a NASA bulletin; the term *nerukotvornyi* (Greek *acheiropoietos*), applied to a miraculous icon, has to be paraphrased. Yet the translation draws attention to some of the hidden problems in a piece so often anthologized and learned by heart in the original Russian that its subtlety becomes blunted. And though workaday English cannot convey the way that Pushkin orchestrates his themes linguistically – with a sound play on 'p' to bring out the grandiose motif of posthumous survival – the dramatism of the piece still comes through.

'Я памятник себе воздвиг нерукотворный'

Exegi monumentum

Я памятник себе воздвиг нерукотворный,
К нему не зарастет народная тропа,
Вознесся выше он главою непокорной
    Александрийского столпа.

Нет, весь я не умру – душа в заветной лире
Мой прах переживет и тленья убежит –

И славен буду я, доколь в подлунном мире
   Жив будет хоть один пиит.

Слух обо мне пройдет по всей Руси великой,
И назовет меня всяк сущий в ней язык,
И гордый внук славян, и финн, и ныне дикой
   Тунгус, и друг степей калмык.

И долго буду тем любезен я народу,
Что чувства добрые я лирой пробуждал,
Что в мой жестокий век восславил я Свободу
   И милость к падшим призывал.

Веленью Божию, о муза, будь послушна,
Обиды не страшась, не требуя венца,
Хвалу и клевету приемли равнодушно
   И не оспаривай глупца.

'I have raised myself a monument not made by human hands'

Exegi monumentum

I have raised myself a monument not made by human hands,
The path of the people to it will never grow over,
Its insubordinate head has risen higher
   Than the Alexandrian Pillar.

No, I shall not fully die – the soul in my fateful lyre
Shall survive my dust, and shall escape putrefaction –
And I shall be famous, wherever in the sublunar world
   Even a single poet lives.

Tidings of me will go out over all great Rus,
And every tribe and every tongue will name me:

The proud descendant of the Slavs, the Finn, the Tungus
    Who is now savage, and the steppe-loving Kalmyk.

And for long I shall remain loved by the people
For awakening noble feelings with my lyre,
Because in my cruel age I have celebrated freedom,
    And called for pity to the fallen.

O Muse, be obedient to the command of God,
Do not be fearful of abuse, do not demand a crown,
Accept both praise and slander with indifference,
    And don't dispute with fools.

Even in English, 'Monument' (to adopt the title commonly, if incorrectly, attached to the poem) gives not only a feeling of 'discovery', but something equally important in a 'classic' text, what Calvino calls 'the sense of rereading something we have read before'. This comes partly from the fact that Pushkin's poem is itself a free translation, or imitation, of an ode by Horace, as the Latin quotation 'Exegi monumentum' makes clear. 'Monument' also plays on an earlier imitation of Horace by the great eighteenth-century poet Gavrila Derzhavin. Derzhavin's poem was both a literal version of Horace and a literal version of the statue motif: Derzhavin's monument has nothing airy or mystical about it, but is 'harder than all metals and taller than the Pyramids'. Pushkin's poem, on the other hand, is teasingly insubstantial: a 'monument not made by human hands' is from some points of view not a monument at all.

In some ways, this idea of an art work about the impossibility of making an art work seems more characteristic of the twentieth century than of the early nineteenth century: it seems Modernist rather than Romantic. But many other themes and motifs in Pushkin's poem – for instance, the idea of dignified survival in the face of a 'cruel age' – evoke the Enlightenment ideals of civilization in whose abstract existence Pushkin fervently believed, even if his own life gave him little chance to experience them in practice. And the theme of art's endurance is common to this poem and to Shakespeare's Sonnet 55, also written under a self-glorifying monarchy ('Not marble, nor the gilded monuments/Of princes shall outlive this powerful rhyme . . .'), while some phrases in 'Monument' play on the finale to Ovid's *Metamorphoses*, hinting at Pushkin's long devotion to Ovid, another poet exiled by a capricious ruler.

'Monument' is not only a quintessential classic, in Calvino's terms, because of its teasing familiarity, but because it 'comes to us bearing the aura of previous interpretations'. Most commonly, the poem is understood as Pushkin's poetic testament. It is one of only a handful of complete poems surviving from 1836, the last year of Pushkin's life, a time during which his existence was made almost unbearable by financial worries, by the struggles to launch his new literary journal *The Contemporary*, and by anxieties aroused by the persistent rumours of his wife Natalya's infidelity – rumours that were to lead directly to Pushkin's death in a duel in January 1837, at the age of only 37. The references to 'dust' and 'putrefaction' can be associated with the emotional contemplation of cemetery scenes that had recurred obsessively in Pushkin's writings from the late 1820s. In this perspective, the fact that the icon of Christ known as 'not made by human hands' was traditionally placed upon Russian graves is certainly of significance.

Yet to see 'Monument' as a kind of 'poetic suicide note' begs the question of the extent to which Pushkin foresaw or willed his own imminent death. It also ignores his long fascination with the monument theme and, more abstractly, what the American Pushkinist David Bethea has termed his 'potential for creative biography', or the self-conscious creation of autobiographical myths. These myths were always elusive and many-faced, and 'Monument' is not at all a straightforward poem. Is Pushkin intending to suggest that only another poet will truly understand his writing? Is the reference to the 'Alexandrian Pillar' (usually taken to mean the Alexander Column, the monument to Alexander I as leader of the Russian forces victorious over Napoleon) simply intended to contrast the miraculous verbal artefact with the inert monument, made to glorify a ruler for posterity, constructed with chisel, pulley, and trowel? (Because the usual term for the 'Alexander Column' is not used, it is possible that Pushkin was, through the term 'Alexandrian Pillar', also referring to the Pharos at Alexandria – and suggesting that his poetry would be the eighth wonder of the world.) And how is Pushkin's pride in speaking to an entire nation compatible with the intense erudition of this poem, whose allusiveness continues to baffle learned commentary?

These questions can be answered in many different ways. A survey of how 'Monument' has been interpreted in different eras of Russian history – as a prophetic evocation in advance of Stalinist literary culture, as an anguished and angry protest by a martyred writer, as a coded message from poet to poet, even as a parody – would shed at least as much light on changing values in Russian culture as on the poem's meaning in its own right. But the importance of 'Monument' goes beyond what it has meant to individual literary critics or even writers. In only five stanzas and twenty lines, the poem raises seven themes of universal resonance in nineteenth- and twentieth-century Russian culture. These are: memorials to the famous as expressions of state power and cultural authority; a writer's 'monument' in the sense of his posthumous reputation; other writers as a writer's ideal readers; a writer's role as teacher to his nation; the writer as a member of polite society; the part played by literature in colonizing, or civilizing, barbarian nations; the relationship between writing and religious experience. These 'signposts' to different themes in Russian literary culture, to ideas and issues that have been of lasting importance in the work of Pushkin's successors, have been used to direct the journey taken in this book.

Following this itinerary does not mean taking on trust the belief, expressed whenever Russians are gathered together to celebrate some anniversary, that 'Pushkin is our all'. Pushkin's celebrated laconicism and lucidity represented only one orientation in literary culture. Many of his successors were inspired not by his finely honed precision, but by the different and in some respects antagonistic conventions of medieval sermons or eighteenth-century odic verse; some spurned written culture altogether in favour of folklore and popular culture. Yet a conscious consideration of how Pushkin worked (even if followed by a repudiation of this) was often or even usually the starting point for the efforts of later authors. And the very fact of the 'Pushkin myth', the obsessive commemoration of the writer in stone and bronze as well as in words, music, in the theatre, or on film, has made it next to impossible to avoid engaging with him. Pushkin is a relatively recent historical presence, and his life, unlike Shakespeare's, is well documented in terms of events, if not in terms of motivation. Therefore, it has become difficult to separate the process of remembering personal history from the commemoration of Russia's national poet, whose presence has dominated the childhood of educated Russians since the late nineteenth century. The best place to begin, then, is where they did: with a monument.

Chapter 2

'I have raised myself a monument'

Writer memorials and cults

> How can I talk about Pushkin? A pygmy riding on a giant.
>
> (Andrey Bely, 1925)

One Russian whose first contact with Pushkin was through a monument was the poet Marina Tsvetaeva. During her childhood in the 1890s, she was regularly taken for walks by her nurse 'to Pushkin's', that is to the Pushkin statue situated on the inner circle of boulevards girding the old centre of Moscow. 'A black man taller and blacker than anyone else', he marked the 'end and bound' of all childhood walks.

The statue represents Pushkin with his head lowered and his hand on his heart, his pose and expression of fierce concentration suggesting he is gripped by inspiration. It is a quintessentially Romantic image, that of the 'improviser' and 'dreamer', which the poet himself evoked in his story 'Egyptian Nights' (1833). Here, a dishevelled and disreputable foreign visitor to St Petersburg has been asked to take part in a sort of literary parlour game. Ladies and gentlemen write down themes on slips, which are then thrown into an urn, and the visitor treats the urn as a sort of lucky dip, pulling out the bits of paper to see what he has to produce a poem about. The subject about which he needs to improvise turns out to be Cleopatra and her lovers:

2. Statue of Pushkin, Pushkin Square, Moscow (A. M. Opekushin, 1880). Much-loved by ordinary Russians, the statue is always decorated with flowers: Lev Tolstoy, who thought it made Pushkin look like a footman announcing 'Dinner is served', was, as usual, expressing an inflammatory view.

> But now the improviser was feeling the approach of his god ... He
> signed to the musicians to begin playing ... His face went fearfully pale,
> and he began shaking as though he were in a fever; his eyes glittered
> with a strange fire; he ran a hand through his black hair, making them
> stand on end, and wiped beads of sweat from his high forehead ... and
> then suddenly took a step forward and crossed his hands on his chest ...
> the music fell silent ... The improvisation had begun.

Here we see an artist in the grip of an acute attack of Romantic
inspiration. Yet it would be unwise to assume that this passage
represents concealed autobiography. Certainly, there is no explicit
invitation in 'Egyptian Nights' to apply this potent myth of divinely
inspired composition to the biographical Pushkin. And the poet's
drafts indicate that his writings, so far from being dashed off at one go,
were worked over intensively and repeatedly before they reached their
finished form. The sophisticated sound effects for which Pushkin strove
required effort, while the complex task of speaking directly and plainly,
and at the same time avoiding excessive baldness, meant that
articulation of a poem's theme or argument became progressively more
allusive in successive versions. But the poet-as-dreamer legend has deep
appeal: Pushkin the painstaking worker has seemed less attractive than
Pushkin the vivacious genius whose every idea was God-given. Later
Russian writers, including Akhmatova and Nabokov, have often worked
with pencil and eraser rather than pen, in order that their first, second,
and forty-fourth thoughts should not become the property of
posthumous disillusion and of meddlesome scholarly enquiry. In the
words of the poet Elena Shvarts (b. 1948), 'There aren't any variants. I
write a poem en bloc. I'm no drudge. Usually I do all the creative work in
the bath'.

If the image chosen for the statue testifies to the lasting hold of
Romanticism on Russian literary culture, the statue's construction was
one milestone in the institution of a Pushkin cult in many ways
comparable with the Shakespeare cult in England. First reflected in

celebrations for the seventieth anniversary of the poet's birth in 1879–80, the cult gathered momentum with the centenary festivities of 1899, and with the hundredth anniversary of the founding of Pushkin's school, the Tsarskoe Selo Lyceum, in 1911, resulting in the production not only of statues and plaques, but of poems, verbal tributes, and paintings. Among the last, remarkable is a vast effort by Ilya Repin, the premier historical painter of the day. It commemorates a famous occasion in 1815, when Pushkin's declamation of his own poem 'Remembrances at Tsarskoe Selo' is said to have induced the elderly Neo-Classical poet Gavrila Derzhavin to hail him as successor. Repin represents the scene as nothing less than a secular icon. Pushkin's pose, and the contrast between his young brilliance and the aged awe of Derzhavin, are based on pictures of the presentation of Christ in the temple, which show the young Jesus astonishing sages with his command of theological debate. But the masks of the listeners – with the exception of Derzhavin, who reaches out to Pushkin – are caricatures of greed, selfishness, and stupidity and are taken from Flemish and Dutch renderings of the mocking of Christ. They hint at the presence of another powerful myth, that of the destruction of artistic talent through the hostile incomprehension of the politically and socially powerful.

Besides its significance in work by sculptors, writers, and painters, the Pushkin cult had, by the 1880s, a commercial undergrowth such as may be seen now at Stratford-upon-Avon or Haworth. To be sure, there were no Prisoner of the Caucasus table-mats, Evgeny and Tatiana mugs, or Bakhchisarai Fountain biscuits, but there were Pushkin pens, Pushkin chocolate-wrappers, Pushkin cigar-boxes, and even Pushkin vodka bottles. Many professional writers and critics, who preferred to see Russian literature as divorced from the marketplace, were shocked and disgusted by the marketing of Pushkin. It seemed one among many symptoms of a culture that was under threat from commercial values. For Sigismund Librovich, who published an album of Pushkin portraits in the wake of the 1889 anniversary, the 'profanation of the poet's beloved

3. Ilya Repin, *Pushkin Reciting his Poem 'Reminiscences of Tsarskoe Selo' at the Lyceum Speech Day, 8 January 1815.*

features' was an illustration of how, 'in the words of Weile, advertising "knows no limits, no respect, honours neither friends nor relations and exploits anything and everything to its own ends"'.

The antipathy of Russian writers to commercialism was a constant of late nineteenth- and early twentieth-century culture; it was to reverberate, for instance, in Nabokov's fulminations against jazz and magazine advertising, and, most creatively, in Humbert Humbert's repelled fascination with American popular culture as represented in *Lolita*. Paradoxically, it was sometimes the most avant-garde and politically radical writers who reacted least allergically to commercial pressures. When Mayakovsky toured Russia giving poetry readings in the mid-1920s, he was quite prepared to harangue the managers of bookshops about their lackadaisical attitude to selling his publications. Cultural centralization in the Soviet Union after 1932 raised the association between commercial culture and low standards to the level of an official dogma. It became a matter of pride that cultural goods (books, paintings, concerts, ballets) were above marketplace values and were available to all at low prices.

To be sure, the means of cultural production, unlike those of industrial production, were never fully nationalized. Publishers were state-owned, but typewriters, paper, pens, and notebooks still had to be purchased; journals accepted contributions from non-unionized writers; royalties continued to be paid, and copyright still existed, though in a restricted form. But the susceptibility of culture to market forces was severely reduced. Authors' royalties depended on prestige (for which read congeniality to the Party authorities) rather than numbers of copies sold; sinecures were paid to established figures who were members of the Writer's Union without regard to how well or even how much they wrote. And commemoration of important authors was always of a 'cultured' kind (to use the Soviet term) – that is, contrived in a manner that could be held to contribute to intellectual self-improvement on the part of the masses. A typical item was a set of post cards intended for

4. A Pushkin-shaped bottle of vodka, produced to mark the centenary of the poet's birth in 1899. The resemblance is, to put it politely, approximate, but using Pushkin's famous features to brand consumable items enraged earnest admirers of the poet, even if (in the case of the item shown here) the poet himself would have consumed them with enthusiasm.

school-leavers, and showing the poet alongside a globe, an array of Pioneer and Komsomol badges, and the complete works of Lenin. It was possible to buy a Pushkin bust, a miniature of the Pushkin monument, or a Tales of Pushkin brand chocolate, but T-shirts with Pushkin on them, or comic-book versions of *Evgeny Onegin*, were emphatically not on sale. On the other hand, cheap editions of Pushkin's works were produced for private reading and for class-teaching, and statues were set up all over the Soviet Union – anywhere that Pushkin had visited for an afternoon had, at the very least, a portrait bust. Museums proliferated everywhere: the practice was gently satirized in Mikhail Zoshchenko's story 'Pushkin' (1927), whose narrator is unable to find a flat in Leningrad from which he is not evicted in short order so that yet another 'museum apartment' can be set up.

Commemoration of other writers, while never as extensively developed as that of Pushkin, was also encouraged by the Soviet state. A museum in Chekhov's Moscow house was opened in 1954; Leningrad acquired a Nekrasov museum in 1946 and a Dostoevsky museum in 1971 (the delay in establishing the last reflected the opprobrium in which the writer was held by the Soviet authorities from the late 1920s until the mid-1950s). A hierarchy of commemoration was established: plaques on the outside of former dwellings for all noteworthy writers, memorial flats for the top tier and second tier of writers, but statues for the top tier alone. In Moscow, for example, there were statues of Dostoevsky (1918), Gogol (1952, replacing an earlier statue), Aleksandr Ostrovsky (1929), Gorky (1951), and Tolstoy (1956). Soviet writers similarly honoured included Mayakovsky (1958), A. N. Tolstoy (the 'Soviet count', whose statue went up in 1957), and Aleksandr Fadeev (long-time General Secretary of the Soviet Writers' Union, who committed suicide after Khrushchev's denunciation of Stalin in 1956; his monument was put in place in 1972). 'Museum flats' included those of, besides the writers already mentioned, the Soviet novelist Nikolay Ostrovsky, author of the factory novel *How the Steel was Tempered* (1935). The memorial plaques are too numerous to list.

Another and more macabre kind of honorific gesture – one emphasizing the importance of death cult for the Soviet state – was the exhumation of famous writers from their original resting places. Levered up from the graves of their families, they were reburied in pantheon-cemeteries for the famous, notably the 'Literary Walks' in Leningrad. (From this indignity, Pushkin, intriguingly, was spared, perhaps because of the resonant disgust for urban cemeteries that is expressed in some of his late poems. He remained in the Svyatogorsky Monastery near the family estate of Mikhailovskoe in northwestern Russia, while his wife Natalya was allowed to continue lying next to her second husband in the graveyard attached to the Alexander Nevsky monastery in Leningrad-St Petersburg.)

There is an obvious link between the treatment of writers' remains and the 'translation', or removal to a new site, of relics that was a requisite step in the creation of the cult of an Orthodox saint. Reverence for writers was a form of secular religion, and the materialism that was a central dogma of Marxism-Leninism expressed itself in a literal-minded determination that memorials should actually enshrine the dust of the departed. The connection between religion and literature was also brought home by the arrangements for the 1937 jubilee, described in advance by the newspaper *Izvestiya*: 'A gigantic portrait of Pushkin reading his poems will be installed at the top of the belfry of the former Strastnoy Convent. The façade of the convent will be covered with a magnificent panel depicting a Soviet youth demonstration, with the marchers shown carrying books by Pushkin and portraits of the leaders.' The Convent of Christ's Passion (the meaning of the name 'Strastnoy'), was not chosen as a focus for the celebrations simply because of its convenient location next to the Pushkin statue, but because its dedication made it a suitable place for commemorating the life of Russia's most important poetic martyr.

The blatancy with which literature was presented as an alternative religion (and the association of this, during the Stalin era, with the ruler's own 'cult of personality') was perhaps the only peculiarly 'Soviet' aspect of post-revolutionary writers' cults. In many other ways, these simply perpetuated the past. Literary museums as well as statues had begun to multiply before the Revolution: an example was Tolstoy's Moscow house, opened to the public as early as 1911, a year after the writer's death. And 'museum apartments' remained popular places for self-educating visits in the post-Soviet period too. Indeed, the years after 1991 saw the founding of numerous museums as the result of private initiative (for instance, in the apartment once inhabited by Anna Akhmatova in the Sheremetiev Palace, St Petersburg, or the house where Marina Tsvetaeva lived in the Arbat district of Moscow). The bi-centenary of Pushkin's birth in 1999 may have had commercial spin-offs of a kind not witnessed for a hundred years (such as the reappearance of Pushkin vases and Pushkin matchboxes) as well as some never seen before (for instance, an Internet 'postcard' showing Pushkin kicking Danthès in the nether regions and then kissing Natalya). But it was also marked by a crop of entirely conventional monuments – such as a hideous gilded statue of Pushkin and his wife in the Moscow Arbat, with the poet shown slightly taller than Natalya, rather than a head shorter, as he was in reality. (Ill. 6.)

The capacity of writer cults to withstand historical vicissitude has been striking. Monuments and memorials to authors not only survived the revolutionary iconoclasm of the first decade of Soviet rule, but stayed in place during later statue-toppling frenzies as well. Dostoevsky's effigy remained in its position outside his birthplace throughout the Stalin years; A. N. Tolstoy, an instrument and beneficiary of literary Stalinism, was spared from the post-1961 monument purge that rid Soviet cities of images of his master; Fadeev, an assiduous signer of arrest-warrants during the Great Terror, went on standing on his pedestal when the memorial to Feliks Dzerzhinsky, the founder of the Soviet secret police, was torn down by Muscovites protesting against the coup by hardline Communists in August 1991. The only exception to the general rule of conservation was the museum flat of Nikolay Ostrovsky, part of which was turned in the late 1990s into an exhibition of waxworks. But this one instance most certainly did not point to a decline in reverence for literary figures in general.

The commemorative efforts of twentieth-century British lovers of literature (discreet blue plaques on London houses and the like) pale into insignificance before Russian ones. Different, too, is the place of the memorials in popular culture. It would be, to put it mildly, unusual if a couple decided to begin their honeymoon with a visit to Stratford (as a Russian couple might with a visit to Pushkin's estate in Mikhailovskoe);

even the most famous writers' museums (for instance, the Brontë house in Haworth) attract a less socially diverse group of visitors than their Russian equivalents. What is more, the existence of commemorative cults has, since the late nineteenth century, been what the Formalist scholar Yury Tynyanov termed a 'literary fact', that is, a point in real life that is of significance to literary composition.

Writers varied considerably in their attitudes to the memorialization of their predecessors, and to the possibility that they might one day themselves be memorialized. For some early twentieth-century poets, for example Innokenty Annensky and Anna Akhmatova, evoking a statue was a way of emphasizing continuity between past and present. Both poets imagined Pushkin's bronzes coming back to life, walking among the avenues of Tsarskoe Selo that he had celebrated in his poetry. Later, Akhmatova was to conclude her poetic commemoration of the Great Terror, *Requiem*, with a reference to the time when the poet's own memorial might be placed outside the Leningrad central

5. Graffiti showing Woland from *The Master and Margarita* in 'Margarita's house', Moscow. An instance where literary characters have become part of popular culture.

prison, Kresty. The statue would be a perpetual admonition to the city's population of the tragedy that *Requiem* itself commemorated:

> And let the melted snow stream
> Off the immobile, bronze eyelids,
>
> And let the prison dove coo in the distance,
> And the ships peacefully sail down the Neva.

Akhmatova was also to allude in some of her work to the custom of naming streets after famous writers, as a way of raising the question of what traces her life would leave in the future. So too was the poet Osip Mandelstam in the bleak days of exile in 1935, when physical survival came to seem more and more unlikely:

> Whichever street is this?
> Mandelstam Street.
> What sort of damn name is that?
> However you turn it about
> It sounds crooked, not straight.
>
> The street was crooked, not straight,
> And he was black, not white, in his ways,
> That's why this street,
> Or, rather, this pit –
> Has its name:
> After that Mandelstam.

The fictional Mandelstam Street has acquired its name by a grotesque reversal of the usual process by which such names were assigned. A side-street instead of a main one has been picked, and instead of conferring immortality and transcendence, it recalls death and constriction. The word 'pit' (*yama*) is used for a communal grave, such as those in which prisoners in labour camps were buried, and is also a colloquial term for the prison itself. The street is an alley in hell, not a thoroughfare in the socialist heaven. The only detail that mimics official procedure is that the course of the street stands for the life-course of the person commemorated, but as both are 'crooked', the result is improper in two ways at once.

Yet if Mandelstam's poem travestied the idea of street-naming to suggest the marginal place of this particular writer in his culture, it still took as a given the link between the monument and the artistic biography. It was only at less forbidding points of Soviet history that writers could afford to distance themselves from the idea of a physical afterlife. In a poem from his last collection, *When the Sky Clears* (1956–9), written during the so-called 'Thaw' era that followed the death of Stalin, Boris Pasternak was to repudiate the notion of turning oneself into a piece of living heritage:

> To be famous is unattractive.
> That is not what elevates.
> One should not start up an archive,
> Fuss over one's manuscripts.
>
> The end of creation is self-surrender,
> Not noise, and not success.
> It is disgraceful to be worthless,
> Yet a name in everyone's mouth.

By the late Soviet period, the greatest reward that a recognized writer such as Pasternak could imagine was being allowed to live out his life in decent obscurity. But what one of Pasternak's biographers has termed his 'choreographed self-effacement', the elusiveness that he shared with Western Modernist poets such as T. S. Eliot, Robert Frost, or Elizabeth Bishop, was relatively rare in a culture where writers risked being effaced whether they wished it or not. A much more customary strategy was the grandiose rejection of official commemoration and the substitution of a magnificently egotistical alternative cult of self. Vladimir Mayakovsky's superb elegy for the poet Sergey Esenin, composed after the latter committed suicide in 1925, and one of the greatest poems written in Russian in the twentieth century, contains an extraordinary passage that at once repudiates the official construction of monuments and builds a monument before the reader's eyes:

> They haven't even
> > built you a memorial,
> No bronze rings out,
> > no stone lies hewn in hunks,
> But the rails of memory
> > are ornamented
> With tributes and with memoirs –
> > all that junk.

By a staggering lapse in historical diplomacy, a particularly absurd and tasteless bronze Esenin was set up in 1995 (the centenary of the writer's birth) not far away from the central Moscow Pushkin statue. So 'the raising of monuments' to writers, in the teeth of opposition from writers, went on.

Perhaps 'staggering' is the wrong word, given that the poem the constructors of the Pushkin statue in Moscow had the gall to inscribe upon its pedestal was, of all poems, 'Monument', which, after all, precisely opposes the living memorial of poetry and the dead weight of stone. It turns out to be the iconoclastic Mayakovsky who wrote most in Pushkin's own spirit, then, recognizing that the elevation of statues to writers was unlikely to be compatible with an appreciation of the dynamic force in their writing. In a culture where the physical presence of the monument can seem extraordinarily daunting, it has been vital to tear Pushkin free from stone and turn him into an airy space for imaginative fantasy. Thus, in Mikhail Bulgakov's play *The Last Days* (1934–5), a representation of the events leading to Pushkin's fatal duel with Danthès, Pushkin himself remains perpetually just off-stage, becoming a creation in the minds of those who talk about him outside the door of his study and in the salons of St Petersburg, and also of the second audience watching beyond, in the auditorium.

Yet, as Bulgakov's play also recognized, the absence of a great writer could be as powerful a cultural force as his presence. The avant-garde's desire to 'throw Pushkin, Tolstoy and Dostoevsky off the steam-ship of modernity', as expressed in the notorious Cubo-Futurist manifesto *A Slap in the Face of Public Taste* (1912), assaulted the status of great writers, but perpetuated this by seeing them as the central symbols of their age. And the equivocality of most assaults upon Pushkin and other famous writers of the past could only be increased by the occasional attacks in another key, such as those of the radical critic Dmitry Pisarev in the 1860s. Pisarev's riposte to a line from Pushkin's 'The Poet and the Mob', 'They sell the Apollo Belvedere by weight' had been to question the utility of art works in the first place. Addressing an anonymous and imaginary follower of Pushkin, he expostulated: 'As for you, elevated cretin, son of the heavens, what do you heat your food in, a cooking-pot or the Apollo Belvedere?' Here the statue, like Pushkin himself, became a metaphor for the inadequacy, in utilitarian terms, of artistic activity in general, an association that could only strengthen, among those in any sense committed to art, the widespread identification between cult and writer, monument and literary function.

The subject of this chapter has been the monuments of writers in the most literal sense – statues, museums, plaques on walls – and with the ways in which these are given meaning by governments, by spectators, and by other writers. In the next chapter, we will move on to look at writers' monuments in another sense: their actual writings, and the ways in which these are presented to posterity, both by writers and by members of the literary establishment, publishers, critics, and censors, which last had such a vital, though obscured, role in the development of Russian literature.

6. Double statue of Pushkin and Natalya, unveiled for the bicentenary in 1999, Arbat, Moscow.

Chapter 3
'Tidings of me will go out over all great Rus'
Pushkin and the Russian literary canon

He embraced the entire world with his soul, both East and West.

(Vera Panova, *A Writer's Notes*, 1972)

The idea that his writings would be his 'monument' was not something that Pushkin regarded merely as a soothing fantasy in the midst of unbearable isolation. It was also something that he tried to ensure in a practical way. He was one of the first Russian writers to assemble his scattered publications into a *Collected Works*, whose content and layout he planned carefully, revising some of his early poems for inclusion. In Russia, such care over the dissemination of one's poems was decidedly new. Until the late seventeenth century, textual production was dominated by the Orthodox Church, and writers fulfilled much the same function as icon-painters. Many texts (for example, prayers) circulated anonymously, and authors had no control over copying procedures or over the use of their materials in compilations. It was the saintliness or theological expertise of writers that gave their work value, even if rhetorical force played a part in establishing this. Things did not change immediately with the introduction of print in the seventeenth century, given that the new technology was at first used for the production of religious books. Once a secular print culture did come into being, during the eighteenth century, titles were at first more important than authors: translated texts were regularly published anonymously, or wrongly credited, and plagiarism and book piracy were rife.

In the late eighteenth and early nineteenth centuries, though, a number of changes came about. Book censorship, tightened up successively under Catherine II, Paul I, Alexander I, and Nicholas I, underlined the concept of individual authorship. This was not only because authors were held responsible for what they wrote and anonymity was strongly discouraged (the publication of unsigned journal articles was expressly forbidden in 1848). It was also because, alongside their punitive role, censorship boards were responsible for enforcing copyright. In the words of an official edict, they were supposed to 'prevent publishers from the unauthorized and capricious publication of books by authors with whom those publishers have no connection'. At the same time, the growth of self-consciousness was fostered by the emergence of the censor as a reader who was assumed to be both hostile and artistically literate (several prominent nineteenth-century censors, including Ivan Goncharov, the author of *Oblomov*, the famous novel about a character who can't get out of bed, were themselves writers). The need for writers to keep ahead of censors stimulated authors into different forms of allegorical writing. For instance, a tale would be set at the Spanish court, when the Russian one was meant, or references to *Hamlet* and the rottenness of the state of Denmark would be used to suggest somewhere much closer to home. This use of what was termed 'Aesopian language' by writers also encouraged readers (and, of course, censors) to read between the lines of texts, searching for hidden meanings.

Also in the early nineteenth century, booksellers became aware of the value of authorial 'brand names' in the marketplace. They began to enter into contracts according to which the grant to a publisher of

ЕВГЕНІЙ ОНѢГИНЪ,

РОМАНЪ ВЪ СТИХАХЪ.

СОЧИНЕНІЕ

АЛЕКСАНДРА ПУШКИНА.

САНКТПЕТЕРБУРГЪ.

ВЪ ТИПОГРАФІИ ДЕПАРТАМЕНТА НАРОДНАГО
ПРОСВѢЩЕНІЯ.

1825.

7. Front cover of *Evgeny Onegin: Chapter One.*

The front cover of the first chapter of *Evgeny Onegin*, first published in 1825. Pushkin's 'novel in verse' is widely regarded as his highest achievement; some, such as Vladimir Nabokov, have considered it the greatest novel in Russian literature. The haunting tale of how Tatiana, an imaginative young woman from a family of small landowners in the Russian provinces, falls in love with Evgeny, a sophisticated, blasé St Petersburger with Byronic aspirations, but finds her feelings reciprocated only when she is no longer able or willing to return them, has alternately provoked and enraptured readers by its simultaneous defiance and assertion of convention, its combination of deep emotion and ironic non-committal. Evgeny and Tatiana, especially the latter, were precursors of many later characters in Russian novels, from Turgenev's Liza in *Nest of Gentlefolk* to Tolstoy's Anna Karenina and Nabokov's Ada. The book also has at least two other niches in literary history. As a text set in a time before that in which it was actually written, it is, in a sense, the first great Russian historical novel. It was also a pioneering example of the serial novel, published chapter by chapter over seven years (1825–32) and appearing in complete form only in 1833. This piecemeal method of publication was later to be used for many other famous works, among them *War and Peace* and *Crime and Punishment* (though the instalments of these novels came out in journals, rather than in book form). In the course of serial publication, writers' views of characters sometimes changed; they, and their readers, tended to see this positively, feeling that it gave their fictional creations the inconsistency and inscrutability of real people. It was rare for writers to make major changes to individual episodes before the book version came out: as Pushkin put it in the first chapter of *Evgeny Onegin*, 'There are many contradictions/But I don't want to correct them'.

exclusive rights to a text or collection of texts was rewarded by the sharing of profits between himself and the writer. In 1834, Pushkin entered into such an agreement with A. F. Smirdin for a book of whose commercial success both had high hopes, the historical novel *The Captain's Daughter*. And in 1836 he started a literary journal, *The Contemporary*, which offered him, as well as the chance of commercial returns, a forum for his writings and direct control over the manner in which these appeared.

One thing that Pushkin took authorship to mean, then, was the careful regulation by individuals of the manner in which their utterances came before the public. He also saw writing as an occupation which, though not exactly gentlemanly, at any rate helped raise the income necessary to a gentleman's existence. But writing was also understood by him as cultural leadership. That Russia needed a literature equal in standing to that of France, Germany, or England, and that there existed no native literary tradition worth the name, were defining assumptions for Pushkin and his generation of Russian writers. In their view, the Russian literary landscape resembled the 'empty waves', gloomy forests, and boggy lichen-covered shores of the unimproved North that Pushkin evoked in the prologue to *The Bronze Horseman* (1833). Monotony, rather than chaos, was the precedent and stimulus to creation. 'We have neither a literature nor [good] books', Pushkin grandly asserted in 1824. Though he allowed merit to various predecessors, including Derzhavin and Ivan Krylov (best-known for his lively and vigorous fables), it was clear none of these was a 'natural genius' (*Naturgenie*) in the Romantic sense, or for that matter a national genius. In an essay written a year later, Pushkin explicitly denied the right of the brilliant scientist and pioneering poet Mikhailo Lomonosov to be recognized in this capacity, presenting him instead as a mere craftsman: 'For him poetic composition was a pastime, or, as more often, an exercise undertaken out of a stern sense of duty [. . .] In our first poet we would look in vain for flaming bursts of feeling or imagination.'

8. Front cover of *Apollo*, no. 6, 1913.

The title page of *Apollo* (no. 6, 1913). Journals played an enormously important role in the publication of Russian literature from the late eighteenth century until the late twentieth. Pushkin's *The Contemporary*, itself the successor to magazines such as *The Drone* and *The European Herald*, was followed by dozens of organs of all political hues. Soviet literary history naturally emphasized the role of radical journals, but conservative ones, such as *The Russian Herald* (which serialized works by both Tolstoy and Dostoevsky) had at least equal distinction. The illustration here shows the frontispiece of one of the most important Modernist journals. At this period, literary magazines rebelled against the drab presentation formerly considered proper for serious publications. Beautifully designed and printed, and copiously illustrated, they, and their successors in the 1920s, are unique in Russian history as total works of art. From the early 1930s, Soviet magazines again reverted to the visual mediocrity current in the nineteenth century (and emphasized by the dreadful quality of paper and typefaces in use).

These observations proceeded from silent questions about Pushkin's own place in Russian literary culture; they showed him moving to a comprehension that it might be possible to make himself the national poet whose lack was so strongly felt. Taking issue with a view expressed by a contemporary, according to which great poets came out of nowhere and vanished into nothing, their glory being followed by an inevitable decadence, Pushkin argued, rather, that an age of mediocrity might be the necessary preparation for the work of great writers. Had not Herodotus preceded Aeschylus, and Catullus Ovid? Though good manners precluded a direct statement of the appreciation that Derzhavin and Pushkin might stand in the same relation, after 1825

Pushkin occasionally began to represent himself as Poet rather than poet – as the priest chosen by Apollo in a famous poem of 1827, for example. But his view of himself was always ambivalent (as suggested by a doodle in the margin of a draft of his Oriental poem *Tazit* (1830): a self-portrait bust with a laurel wreath has been fiercely scored out in thick black ink). It was other commentators who, especially after Pushkin's tragic death in 1837, were with growing confidence to claim for him the greatness to which he had tentatively aspired. A signal moment was when the prolific and influential critic Vissarion Belinsky declared in 1838, 'Every educated Russian must have a complete Pushkin, otherwise he has no right to be considered either educated or Russian'.

Interpretations of this kind naturally came to the forefront at the various Pushkin jubilees. The speeches made by writers at the raising

9. Pushkin, draft of *Tazit* (1830), with scored-out self-portrait in laurel wreath.

of the Moscow Pushkin monument in 1880, for example, included not only a famous patriotic tirade by Dostoevsky, but also an oration by Turgenev in which he praised Pushkin for combining two achievements that in other countries had occurred at different times and been carried out by different individuals: the creation of a new language and the initiation of a literary tradition. Pushkin's achievement was part of Russia's greatness and a constituent of the country's unique identity.

Turgenev's national triumphalism had shaky foundations in terms of fact. The role played by Goethe in Germany, Mickiewicz in Poland, or Vuk Karadžic in Serbia, was at least as important as that played by Pushkin. Russia's literary upsurge, so far from being unique, was part of a Europe-wide surge into the intellectual mainstream of countries where culture had earlier run in isolated channels. But neither the fragility of Turgenev's case, nor its eccentricity on the part of a writer who spent most of his later life abroad, chattering in French to his famous visitors, discredited his articulation of an idea that was gaining weight as time went on. At the jubilee of 1899, the cult of 'Pushkin as national poet' proved much to the taste of the conservative and nationalist government of Nicholas II. The sponsorship of street renamings and distribution of souvenirs to schoolchildren harnessed Russian writers to official patriotism, and also to the late Imperial Russian government's new-found commitment to educating the Russian masses.

To be sure, the Pushkin cult did not develop unopposed. Tolstoy's famous tract *What is Art?* (1898), for example, poured scorn on the idea of turning a dandy and womanizer such as Pushkin into a national saint. Well before this, in the 1860s, radical critics such as Dmitry Pisarev made Pushkin the spearhead of their assault on Romantic poetry in favour of politically engaged prose. Pisarev used Pushkin's magnificent poem '19 October 1825', with its moving evocation of the literary friendship between the poet and his classmate Wilhelm Küchelbecker, as an illustration of his point that verse was the statement of shallow ideas in unnecessarily complex form: 'If all this rhyming blether is paraphrased as simple and clear prose, then the following thin and pallid message remains: "You and I both used to scribble verses; I used to print mine, and you didn't; and now I'm not going to print mine either."' A fair number of radically minded readers, particularly self-taught intellectuals from the working classes, shared Pisarev's reservations. 'Your Onegin and your Lensky [. . .] should have been sent to a factory to fit cylinders to a vice', one memoirist recalled his workmates saying in the 1910s. For readers of this kind, Maxim Gorky's propaganda novel *The Mother* (1906), about a simple woman brought to political enlightenment by the cruelty of the Tsarist authorities, was a great deal more moving than *Evgeny Onegin*.

These scruples had a powerful institutional weight during the first years after the Russian Revolution, when literary-historical scholarship was dominated by the official ideology of 'class war'. For those committed to fighting that war, Pushkin was no more than a supremely gifted member of a reactionary cultural elite. Most so-called 'leftists', too, were admirers of fiction (especially Realist fiction), not of 'rhyming blether'. Significantly, the first writers whose biographies appeared in *The Lives of Famous People*, an uplifting series for the mass market that began publication at the instigation of Gorky in 1933, were Chekhov, Gogol, the eighteenth-century radical dissident Aleksandr Radishchev, and the satirist Saltykov-Shchedrin, scourge of the privileged classes, rather than Pushkin. Similarly, the keynote speeches at the 1934 Congress of Soviet Writers emphasized the pre-eminence, alongside the Realist fiction of Gorky and of Tolstoy, of 'progressive' critics such as Belinsky, Nikolay Chernyshevsky, and Nikolay Dobrolyubov. As late as 1949, a list of required reading for the Soviet masses put forward by the Party leader, Old Bolshevik, and former worker Mikhail Kalinin consisted of Lomonosov (as an example of the supreme auto-didact and scientific genius), the 'revolutionary moralist' Radishchev, Belinsky, and Dobrolyubov, with the radical poet Nikolay Nekrasov the sole example of an imaginative writer.

Right until the end of the Soviet era, 'progressiveness' – which is to say, the holding of views that could be represented as foreshadowing Soviet ones – was the primary criterion by which work by dead writers was judged as fitting, or not, for acknowledgement as 'classic literature'. 'Progressiveness' was to be found in Chernyshevsky's plodding, formulaic novel of women's liberation, *What is to be Done?* (1863), but not in Dostoevsky's *The Devils* (1871–2), which the second edition of *The Great Soviet Encyclopedia* labelled a 'virulent slur upon the Russian movement for political liberation'. It was to be found in Tolstoy's *War and Peace*, but only to a much more limited degree in *Anna Karenina* (decidedly a novel of the second rank, from an official Soviet point of view, because of the unfortunate prominence in it of adulterous passion). It was evident in Nekrasov's socially critical poetry, but most definitely not in the 'idealist' works of Russian Symbolism and post-Symbolism. It was evident in radical periodicals of high principle but decidedly modest literary merit, such as *The Spark*, but not in the artistically ambitious (and politically liberal) Modernist journals of the early twentieth century, such as *Apollo* or *The Scales*. Accordingly, it was selections from the former journal, and not the latter two, that appeared in the 'Poet's Library', the most prestigious series of retrospective editions of poetry, published by the leading house 'The Soviet Writer'.

Emphasis upon 'progressiveness' had especially piquant results where eighteenth-century literature was concerned. That the reign of the 'reactionary' Catherine II (herself one of the first Russian women writers) had been a far more productive era for Russian letters than that of the 'progressive' Peter I was bad enough; far more embarrassing was the conservatism of most Russian writers themselves, who were much more likely to pen court odes celebrating autocracy than to attack serfdom. As a result, much eighteenth-century Russian literature was simply not republished between the early 1930s and the late 1980s, and treatments of the period for the mass market (unlike those published between the 1890s and the 1920s) concentrated on a bare handful of figures. Apart from Radishchev and Lomonosov, the rarefied company of acceptable writers included the literary journalist Nikolay Novikov (mythologized as a martyr of Catherine II's political censorship). Nikolay Karamzin, on the other hand, was branded a 'gentry sentimentalist', and a good deal of his work remained under wraps: his masterful *History of the Russian Empire* (1818–29), for instance, was not republished in full until the late 1980s. To grasp the eccentricity of this, one might imagine a list of eighteenth-century English greats consisting of Tom Paine, Mary Wollstonecraft, and the early Wordsworth, but excluding Pope, Johnson, Fanny Burney, and Thomson on the grounds of their questionable politics, and Swift on the grounds of his questionable propriety. (As a matter of fact, in the Stalin years *Gulliver's Travels* was published as a children's book, in heavily abridged form.) So far as nineteenth-century English literature goes, it is not necessary to imagine a canon of 'progressive' writers, because one was actually constructed by the efforts of Soviet translators. It consisted of Shelley (the pioneering atheist and democrat), Burns (the 'people's poet' of Scotland), William Blake (as the denouncer of 'satanic mills' rather than as visionary mystic), and – as the towering figure – Dickens. It most certainly did not include Jane Austen (translated only from the late 1950s), George Eliot (who had been extremely popular in nineteenth-century Russia), or Emily Brontë, let alone Gerald Manley Hopkins or Christina Rossetti.

The canon of 'progressive' writers was at once static and flexible. Some writers, such as Tolstoy, maintained their pre-eminence from the beginning to the end of Soviet power; others, such as Pushkin, underwent a marked change in status. The most crucial stage of reassessment came in the mid-1930s, when 'class war' was decreed to have ended and there was a move to conservatism in terms of family and educational policy (a set of changes collectively known as 'the Great Retreat'). Along with structural changes went symbolic changes: with increasing emphasis on the fact that cultural values transcended social circumstances went a resurgence of 'classic' styles in architecture, music, and painting. Not coincidentally, too, the Lenin cult instituted upon the leader's death in 1924 began to subside in favour of an emphasis upon 'Soviet patriotism', centred round figures whose glory reflected and enhanced that of the 'coryphaeus of all knowledge', Stalin himself. The centenary of Pushkin's death in 1937 came at a crucial stage in this set of processes, and was itself used in order to enforce a new, and entirely circular, identification of artistic merit and political progressiveness.

During the 1920s, Pushkin had been perceived as an artist of supreme talent but dubious opinions; from 1937, he began to be seen as an

10. Aleksey Remizov, 'A Dream of Pushkin' (1937).

Aleksey Remizov, 'A Dream of Pushkin' (1937). For the different communities of Russian émigrés forced to settle abroad after the Revolution, Pushkin and his works had poignant significance. Émigrés wanted to defend the writer from the distastefully tendentious attention that he was receiving inside the Soviet Union, but were frustrated by lack of access to Pushkin's manuscripts. However, B. L. Burtsev's call in 1934 for 'the publication abroad of a new edition of Pushkin's *Complete Works*, or at the very least, of individual editions of his major works' had a belated response in Vladimir Nabokov's commentary on *Evgeny Onegin*, one of the greatest achievements of twentieth-century interpretive scholarship. And anniversaries (particularly the centenary of Pushkin's death in 1937) were celebrated by conferences and exhibitions, while Pushkin's writings remained, as always, an important inspiration for writers and artists. This fantasy sketch by the writer Aleksey Remizov shows Pushkin as a benevolently demonic presence, in tune with Symbolist emphasis on demonism in his writings.

artist of supreme talent and utterly sound opinions, a vehement opponent of serfdom and a thorn in the side of autocracy. His modest literary magazine, *The Contemporary*, was conflated with its successor, the politically committed journal run under that name by Nekrasov and others in the 1840s and 1850s. It became customary to emphasize the importance of his relations with the organizers of the Decembrist Rebellion in 1825, and to stress his admiration for dissident writers. With much pomp and ceremony, a draft version of 'Monument' was published in the journal of the Pushkin Commission in 1937. It inidcated that the original version of the final stanza had contained the line, 'I followed Radishchev in hymning freedom'. This cancelled line had long been known to scholars, and is no less ambiguous than everything else in the poem (one possible interpretation, since Radishchev was a famous suicide, is that Pushkin was evoking the 'freedom' he had exercised in ending his own existence). The fact that it was cancelled, too, makes interpretations based solely upon it rather dubious. But, in pious evocations of the progressive Pushkin, it acquired the status of a last, rather than a first, word. As one commentator put it in 1962: 'Only in 1937, upon the centenary of Pushkin's tragic death, did the genuine meaning of his "testament" become clear.'

Nothing was allowed to disturb the presentation of Pushkin as a 'forward-thinking' figure. A popular edition of Pisarev's essays on literature published in 1940 simply omitted the essay 'Pushkin's Lyric Poetry' in which the quotation about 'rhyming blether' cited earlier in this chapter appeared. The piece was made available only in more ambitious editions, such as Pisarev's *Works* of 1955–6. Equally, Pushkin's unmistakable turn to political conservatism after 1830 – his defence of serfdom and growing conviction that autocratic rule was essential to the dissemination of enlightenment – was not an acceptable subject of discussion for Soviet specialists. And in its turn, the fact that Pushkin was now deemed 'the founding father of magnificent Russian literature', a kind of literary equivalent to Peter I, contributed to the eclipse of the eighteenth century: founding fathers have by definition no need of ancestors.

Another aspect of the 'founding father' cult was that Pushkin increasingly became the subject of overt chauvinism. The theme of 'Pushkin as ultimate genius' was already an undertone in the Pushkin jubilee of 1937. It made itself felt in translation policy. A table published in 1945 set out the following tally of languages into which various great writers had been rendered before and after the Revolution:

Writer	Languages into which translated before 1917	After 1917
Pushkin	9	66
Tolstoy	10	54
Chekhov	5	53
Lermontov	5	26
Saltykov-Shchedrin	1	24
Nekrasov	1	21
Romain Rolland	1	13
Goethe	1	6

The theme rose to the height of a trumpet blast at the 150th anniversary of Pushkin's birth in 1949, which coincided with the onset of the Cold War and the beginning of an anti-Semitic and xenophobic campaign against 'rootless cosmopolitanism'. Two lectures (also published as booklets) by a member of the Academy of Sciences represented the writer as a figure who, while 'soaking up everything that was best in preceeding culture, both Russian and foreign', had been filled with 'national pride' and had presciently 'lambasted cosmopolitanism', as well as 'aestheticism and formalism'. Naturally, the appreciation that 'cosmopolitanism' was shameful was to be a powerful impediment to analysis of such issues as Pushkin's vexed but intimate relationship with Western Romantic literature. So, too, the belief that Russian literature was of particular and extraordinary value and character impeded analysis of the Russian contribution to European-wide movements such as the cult of sensibility or Modernism. Between 1948 and 1956, there was little or no serious discussion of such topics. The admiration of the Russian radicals for *Evgeny Onegin*, which Belinsky grandly, if inaccurately, held to have 'exhausted the whole of Russian life', was adduced as proof positive of Pushkin's mature appreciation of

Romanticism's limitations. The fact that the novel's ambivalent treatment of Romantic emotions and character types was perfectly in accordance with the practices of 'Romantic irony' (compare the work of Byron or Heinrich Heine) was ignored. And the resemblance of Pushkin's novel *The Captain's Daughter* to Walter Scott's *Redgauntlet*, where rebellion by the oppressed succeeds only in substituting an unreliable tyranny for an authoritarianism in which reason plays some part, was overlooked in interpretations which made the novel into an unambiguous critique of Catherine II's 'bestial' suppression of the peasant rebel Pugachev.

The other important ambition of the Stalinist regime, apart from presenting Pushkin as an ancestor of Soviet literature and instrument of national suprematism, was to present him as a 'national writer' in the sense of 'national-popular': a writer for the entire nation. Already in the 1920s, there had been a wide-ranging drive aimed at giving new readers a chance to make their first acquaintance with the Russian classics. Reader surveys anxiously monitored the reactions of proletarians and peasants to these. The surveys themselves produced very diverse responses, but analyses of them generally boiled the material down to make a straightforward case: Modernism was incomprehensible to ordinary people, while the classics were accessible to everyone. As a Russian peasant woman was said to have commented in a survey of 1926, 'And "Monument"? How could you not feel something after that?'.

Statements of this kind were meant not just to report opinion, but to shape it. This was the kind of reaction that Soviet 'mass readers' were *supposed* to have when reading great literature. Accordingly, the authorities made sure to provide them with the kind of literature likely to induce such responses. From the mid-1930s, the Russian classics again became the core of literature teaching in schools, and instruction focused on material that was both accessible and morally uplifting. Pupils had to learn by heart Tatiana's letter from *Evgeny Onegin* (Tatiana

11. V. Klutsis, poster for the Pushkin Jubilee of 1937. The poem in the open book appears to be 'Monument'.

was considered a role-model for Soviet womanhood), and Turgenev's prose poem to 'the great and magnificent Russian language'. Rather than the psychologically complex and embittered verse that Lermontov had written in his final years, or the scathing poems in which the writer complained that it was 'painful to survey his generation' and bid an unfond farewell to 'unwashed Russia', textbooks included emblematic nature poems evoking the momentous size of the Russian Empire, or such rousing patriotic pieces as 'Two Giants', in which the Russian giant defeats his foreign rival, and 'Borodino', evoking the Russian defeat of Napoleon in 1812. The result was that from childhood, Russian readers carried round a treasured mental anthology of poems such as these, and a knowledge of prose classics taught in the classroom (for example, Gogol's 1841 tale of the miserable civil servant Akaky Akakievich, *The Overcoat*).

The interpretation of great writers was as limited as the selection of their works offered for study. Pupils had to write moralistic character studies, commenting on Pushkin's Dubrovsky, say, 'He was accustomed to giving free rein to all the stirrings of his fiery spirit'. They had to answer examination questions on 'the significance of Chekhov', which required them to eulogize the writer's prescience in anticipating the Bolshevik Revolution (an event that took place more than 13 years after his death). Formula, rather than independent thought, was essential. As the critic and children's writer Korney Chukovsky observed of Soviet school essays in 1963:

> Every single one, every single one of the classic writers is always described as follows: 1) he loves his motherland; 2) he loves his nation and people; 3) he expostulates against the social abuses of his time; he (like every other classic writer) is 4) a humanist, 5) a realist, 6) an optimist, 7) has no faults and all in all no distinguishing features whatsoever.

Between the late 1930s and the early 1960s, these observations were true by no means only of school essays (of which they continued to be true right up to the collapse of Soviet power), but of writings for a popular auditorium by recognized professional critics and literary historians as well.

Alongside adulation went the suppression of any biographical details that might have proved disruptive, such as Pushkin's fondness for drinking, fornication, gambling, and gooseberry jam, or Tolstoy's predilection for at least three of those four. Gorky's embarrassingly long spell in emigration was also a taboo subject (writers who left Russia after 1917, like other Russian citizens who had gone into exile, were considered by definition to have displayed insufficient 'love of the motherland'). Sexual misdemeanours were an even more prickly point. The lavishly appointed and copiously annotated 'Complete Works' published in the Soviet Union as tribute to the status of first-rank writers rarely quite lived up to their titles. Even if every surviving text a writer had ever penned actually appeared in some form or another, some pieces had certainly been subjected to cuts, not all of which were necessarily as scrupulously signalled as with the asterisks (***** for 'whore' or **** for 'arse', for instance) that replaced words Pushkin himself had brazenly written in full. Piety was equally important in biographical work. As late as 1963, a particularly well-read and reasonably liberal Soviet writer expressed relief that A. L. Rowse, distasteful as his biographical approach might be, had at least 'completely cleared away any suspicion that Shakespeare was a homosexual'. The appropriate manner of writing up the lives of the famous was not unfairly satirized in Aleksandr Solzhenitsyn's novel *Cancer Ward* (1968) as 'exhaustive research about exactly which country path the great poet walked along in eighteen so-and-so' – that is, reportage of events that might be deadly dull, but which were neither politically controversial nor examples of 'salacious triviality' (*poshlyatina*).

After 'vulgar sociologism' was denounced in the late 1930s,

interpretations of Pushkin as 'the poet of the youth of Russian bourgeois culture' (as D. S. Mirsky had called him in 1934) were out of the question. But there was also an end to the intensive study of account books, private letters, diaries, memoirs, and minuscule archival data of all kinds that could have facilitated 'thick description' of writers in the context of their times. Conversely, the work of the Formalist scholars who had protested against 'laundry list' criticism, and against glib categorizations of writers in terms of social class, survived only in diluted form. Studies under titles such as *The Mastery of Gogol* (or any other writer recognized as 'great') acknowledged that at least some aspects of craft, as opposed to ideology, might carry weight. The most sacred literary texts were treated not unlike the speeches of Stalin, who himself was fond of displaying knowledge of the classics, referring, for instance, to supposed 'enemies of the people' as 'Yudushkas' (after Saltykov-Shchedrin's creepy hypocrite Yudushka Golovlyov). They were supposed to be known to everyone, but to discuss them in depth, at any rate without the special licence of a scholar speaking to scholars in an Academy of Sciences research institute, or to cite the wrong works, would have been decidedly imprudent.

The effects of adulation for, and rote-learning of, the classics were not uniformly bad. For a start, learning by heart was not a Soviet invention, any more than literature as a secular religion was. Before the Revolution, schoolchildren had been made to recite authors such as Lomonosov, Pushkin, and Lermontov as part of the secondary-school programme. In the best of circumstances, this gave adult Russians an affectionate familiarity with literature that made it the common currency of cultivation. Nineteenth- and twentieth-century Russian writers (and artists of all kinds) could expect the majority of their readers to recognize literary allusions, sometimes in substantially reworked form. (The importance of intertextuality, that is, direct or indirect quotation, as a subject of study among historians of Russian literature is intimately related to the mental world in which writers grew up.) And though a child who pointed out the relevance to Soviet life of Turgenev's hymn to the 'simple and magnificent Russian language' as the sole domain of freedom in a repressive society ('If you did not exist, how would I not despair?') would have been expelled from the classroom if not the school, there was nothing to stop a pupil enjoying the subversive potential of the piece in private.

Among unsophisticated readers, though, exposure to a 'core curriculum' does not seem to have done much more than perpetuate a sort of literary folklore. It stimulated the circulation of grotesque anecdotes about writers' lives, parodied in the 1930s by the absurdist writer Daniil Kharms, whose 'Anegdotes [*sic*] about Pushkin' contained such pearls of irrelevance as 'Pushkin used to love throwing stones . . .'. Documents such as diaries or letters indicate that the citation of 'winged words', or set phrases, was much more common than the informed reading of classic texts. A young woman who misquoted Lermontov in a letter to her sweetheart ('It is boring and sad, and I have no one's hand to stroke', rather than 'who my hand might take') perhaps did not even know the poem that she was abusing. The tag may have reached her by an intermediate source, such as a popular song.

But the worst side-effect of a system that encouraged school graduates to see the narrow sampling of classic texts to which they had been exposed as the pinnacle of literary endeavour, and to judge every form of writing by that yardstick, was that it promoted aggressive aesthetic conservatism. Rather than knowing nothing about art but knowing what they liked, Soviet philistines thought they knew a good deal about art, and had every right to impose what they liked on others. Large numbers of pupils left school familiar only with what Marina Tsvetaeva called 'Pushkin the perpetual jubiland, whose sole achievement in life was to die', and whose only works were *Evgeny Onegin*, *The Captain's Daughter*, and two or three lyric poems. It is therefore not surprising that the more adventurous texts that did get through censorship often provoked full postbags from a kind of reader one might call 'Disgusted of Tambov' – a provincial school-teacher, engineer, or other member of

12. Design for *The Queen of Spades.*

Design by Mstislav Dobuzhinsky for Stanislavsky's production of Tchaikovsky's opera *The Queen of Spades*. Not only writers but artists of all kinds have been able to take familiarity with Pushkin's work for granted in their audiences. It was quite natural for Eisenstein, in his 1943 book *The Film Sense*, to explain his theories about creative inter-cutting in cinema ('montage') in terms of analogies with Pushkin's poetry. And the fact that film directors, composers, and playwrights could rely on detailed knowledge of Pushkin's plots (or, at any rate, those of his most famous works), much as their British counterparts could in the cases of Shakespeare, Dickens, or Jane Austen, lent them a high degree of freedom when adapting these in new forms. Musorgsky's tormented yet regal Boris Godunov is quite different from Pushkin's ambitious, guilt-ridden version of the character; Tchaikovsky's version of *Queen of Spades* dispenses with the ironic ending of the original story (in which Liza ends up purging her own humiliation as a ward by taking a ward of her own), inserting instead a scene in which Liza does away with herself, in suitably operatic style, by leaping into a canal. At the same time, these outrageous reinterpretations sometimes exposed motifs lying below the surface in the original text. Thus, Tchaikovsky's *Queen of Spades* played on the demonic theme that was kept at one remove by humour and irony in Pushkin. The oversized proportions and looming patterns of Dobuzhinsky's design for the final act are in tune with the composer's intentions.

the Soviet 'petty intelligentsia' appalled that something inimical to the spirit of 'classic Russian literature' in the crippled form that he or she knew it had been published.

The Stalin era, then, saw the development of an exceptionally restrictive canon, not only in the sense that few works were included, but because the manner of discussing these was regulated with extraordinary severity. The cultural liberalization that began in 1954, a year after Stalin's death, was, in this area as in so many others, haphazard and incomplete. It affected, in the main, the scholarly interpretation of Pushkin, but even that only partially. 'Pushkin House', the Institute of Russian Literature of the Academy of Sciences in Leningrad, retained a privileged position with regard to Pushkin publications that has been described by one hostile commentator, not altogether unjustly, as 'a narrow circle of Pushkin priests making monopolistic decisions about whether a particular article served their own ends'. To be sure, the growing diversity that was evident in the publication of literature and of translations began to make itself felt in literary criticism and in scholarship as well. A crucial event was the founding of the Tartu University series *Semiotike* (Studies in Sign Systems), under the leadership of the scholar and critic Yury Lotman in 1965. The concentration of semioticians upon the question of meaning within a given culture at a set time, rather than upon the significance of texts for later generations, mounted a covert challenge to the traditional Marxist-Leninist emphasis upon progressiveness. (It was significant that some of Lotman's best work was devoted to the so-called 'gentry sentimentalist' Karamzin.) The immersion in the past that was required by the semiotic approach also meant that material such as writers' letters and diaries was once again accorded value in itself, as a genre of literary or sub-literary composition, rather than regarded simply as a repository for information about when a writer was doing what to the drafts of his novels, plays, and poems.

However, both in the work of Russian scholars, such as Lotman, and in the work of their Western associates, the material that was considered suitable for investigation was still strictly denominated in some respects. Pushkin's letters to his literary associates were exhaustively analysed, and their playful and watchful crafting of alternative selves recorded, but the writer's letters to his wife and other close relations were not discussed in detail because of the sense the material was 'useful for the biographer' but not for the literary historian, since it had not been meant for publication. The elite world of Russian society was exhaustively analysed: taking their cue from two lines of *Evgeny Onegin*, 'One may be a worthwhile person/And think about having clean nails', semioticians analysed dozens of areas that had been elided by Marxism-Leninism's emphasis on intellectual life, from the 'language of flowers' to the conventions of the duel. Yet gentility was pervasive: though memoirs make it clear that child abuse, incest, rape, violence, as well as less spectacular misdemeanours such as vulgarity and rudeness, were as common in early nineteenth-century Russian society as in any other human community, discussion of such topics was not allowed to disrupt the view of the 'Golden Age' of Pushkin and his contemporaries as an aesthetic paradise. In other words, this was an interpretive tradition that, in seeking to trace the conventions of early nineteenth-century Russian life, often replicated the proprieties against which writers themselves had battled. Even to liberal Russian scholars of this kind, Richard Holmes's life of Coleridge, showing the poet composing his aethereal works in a constant struggle with decidedly earthly afflictions such as constipation, would have seemed trivial and putrid tattle. In some ways, this was a reflection of writers' own determination to transcend physicality. The poet Nikolay Klyuev, desperately sick, bedridden, and a victim of Stalinist persecution, comforted himself with the thought that 'saints can be recognized by their endurance, ability to rise above suffering [. . .] some people's souls are like trumpets, sounding only when catastrophe and the angel of torment blows into them'. Yet the refusal of scholars to interest themselves in personal pain – failed love affairs, divorces, sexual agony – could be obstructive to the study of writers preoccupied, in their work, with precisely these subjects. The Formalist theory that writers self-consciously shaped personal experience as art even while they were living it (termed in Russian *zhiznetvorchestvo*) ignored the fact that some writers were inspired precisely by life's reluctance to subordinate itself to such reshaping (examples of this included some of the women writers discussed in Chapter 6 below).

Even once interest in the 'distinguishing features' of recognized writers proliferated, then, there was little concern with 'faults': rather than 'biography' in the Western sense, the writing of lives meant setting out an author's 'creative path' (the authoritative life of Klyuev eschewed discussion of the poet's homosexual love affairs and concentrated instead upon his artistic relationships with other writers and with journal editors). The essential task was to represent the life as a saintly path of suffering and triumph (*podvig*): deviations from this model provoked bitter debate, as in the case of the Russian-American critic Alexander Zholkovsky's revisionist interpretation of Anna Akhmatova's biography. Zholkovsky argued that Akhmatova saw her own suffering, political and personal, as a mark of distinction, and strove to emphasize and heighten it. She was not merely an inert and innocent victim, but actively sought out pain. She used others as the instruments of conflict (her history of relationships with men who were already attached to another woman is striking) and as a sounding-board for lamentation (Zholkovsky drew attention to Akhmatova's compulsive desire for an audience, manifested in her repeated commands that her friends should drop everything and rush round to see her when she so required). In a furious response printed in *Zvezda*, the literary journal which had published Zholkovsky's article, another Russian-American critic accused Zholkovsky of colluding in, and approving, Akhmatova's oppression: 'Only from a safe distance – whether geographical or chronological – can one write about history and literature with such unruffled alienation from human suffering.' Life-writing was still widely seen as a genre demanding moral engagement and respect bordering on adulation, even when practised by scholars.

If anything, defensiveness about writers' biographies increased in the late 1990s, fuelled by anxiety that Russian literature had lost its traditional hold over Russian culture. In 1998, an essayist writing in the liberal literary journal *Kontinent* cited, as one of a list of accusations aimed at demonstrating the 'unculturedness' of the Russian media, the fact that Russian television had marked the occasion of 'Pushkin Day', an official festival instituted by Boris Yeltsin in that year, only by the showing of 'some kind of parody ballet performed by half-naked avant-garde dancers'. The accusation against the media was strikingly unfair, given that the build-up to the bicentenary of the writer's birth in 1999 was actually marked by dozens of reverential programmes. But it showed Pushkin becoming the figurehead of another kind of conservatism: this time that of a beleaguered intelligentsia who felt that culture was even more under threat in the post-Soviet era than it had been during Soviet rule. In Tatiana Tolstaya's futurist novel *The Mynx* (2000), which shows the inhabitants of a post-nuclear holocaust Moscow condemned for ever to relive Soviet history as farce, an enthusiastic and unlearned book-lover sets up what he calls 'a pushkin', a wooden fetish to some half-forgotten god of the literature that had once existed. But at the same time that it mocks monumentalism, the novel represents knowledge of great writing as a measure of true culture: the perfidy of the post-holocaust dictator and the sterility of the neo-primitive culture he dominates are shown by the fact that he passes off famous poems by Pushkin, Lermontov, and Blok as his own. Once more, the integrity of writing and the writer stands for the moral probity of society at large.

This chapter has dwelled upon the question of the dissemination of literary works in Russia. It began with the issue of writers' control over their own output, a control that was sometimes aided by censorship but more often frustrated by it. Censorship could sometimes act as a stimulus to literary production. More devastating was its effect upon the quality of readership, especially in the Soviet period, when education and publishing for the masses created a new class of self-confident, but rather intellectually limited, readers who took their restricted knowledge of the classics as a measure of aesthetic standards in the absolute. Academic criticism, while based on far broader knowledge of primary material, was itself subject to severe constraints, particularly before 1956. Not only politically explosive material had to be avoided, but also 'vulgar' or 'trivial' themes, a consideration that led to bowdlerization of authors' writings and also to the avoidance of biographical treatments, except where these concentrated on a writer's 'creative path', that is, on intellectual experiences that were relevant to the composition of individual literary texts.

The discussion here should not be taken as meaning that every Russian had to manifest the kind of piety that was expected by school-teachers and government officials in the presence of great writers. As we shall see in the next chapter, many individuals, particularly other writers, had a much bolder attitude to established reputations than that. However, even at the end of the twentieth century, the levels of reverence for classic authors were considerably higher in Russia than they were in Western Europe, let alone America, a situation that was fostered, as well as bedevilled, by the spread of explicitly commercially oriented values in Russian society generally, and in the press in particular.

Chapter 4

'I shall be famous as long as another poet lives'

Writers' responses to Pushkin

> Don't hit me with Pushkin –
> I'll use him to hit you!
> (Marina Tsvetaeva, 1937)

Among commentators on Russian literary history, Pushkin's boast that he would resonate for ever in the minds of poets was sometimes taken at face value, with the poet's work seen as the ultimate source of everything valuable in the work of his successors. But the sense that Pushkin's work was the alpha and omega of all literary endeavour was by no means limited to patriotic bureaucrats or pillars of the educational system. Rather, each successive generation of writers was able to convince itself that it alone had discovered 'the real' Pushkin. This conviction was enhanced by the fact that a great many of Pushkin's writings were not 'Pushkinian' in the sense understood in the schoolroom, but undermined decent commonplaces about balance, restraint, and edification. For example, 'The Drowned Man', a quintessentially Romantic ballad about a revenant taking vengeance on a peasant who has selfishly failed to bury him, starkly evokes the appearance of the ghost:

> The moon rolls out from the rain-clouds –
> What? Naked before him it stands,
> Water running from its beard,

Glare bold and fixed,
Each limb fearfully numb,
And black crayfish fastened
To its swollen body.

As each generation of theatre directors and audiences in the
Anglophone world has constructed its particular Shakespeare (take the
fashion for the so-called 'problem plays' of tortured sexual
relationships, such as *Measure for Measure* and *Troilus and Cressida*, in
the 1960s and 1970s), so successive generations of Russian readers
and critics have discovered 'their' Pushkin. For example, *The
Bronze Horseman*, an evocation of St Petersburg as at once a
supreme art work and a symbol of crushing authoritarianism,
resonated in Petersburg Modernist texts such as Andrey Bely's
novel *Petersburg*, or in a poem by Innokenty Annensky in which the
'yellow fog' of Dostoevsky's novels swirls around the statue hero of
Pushkin's poem.

Given the circumstances of early twentieth-century Russian history, it is
hardly surprising that Pushkin was considered important for what the
religious philosopher Simeon Frank called his 'apprehension of life's
inherent tragedy'. But he was valued also as a writer who had
emphasized the importance of the writer. It was the Romantic side of
Pushkin to which many writers gave weight. The critic Mikhail
Gershenzon felt that 'Monument' was to be interpreted as drawing a
contrast between 'genuine' fame, 'among people who understand
poetry', and 'vulgar fame, among the mob, a muted kind of fame –
mere celebrity'. This interpretation was entirely in the spirit of the
times. Pushkin's poem 'The Prophet', in which the poet was seen as a
Promethean outcast gifted with a uniquely full understanding of his
culture, spawned dozens of imitations between 1890 and 1940 as
Modernist writers reasserted the primacy of art and with it the
Romantic understanding of the artist as hero, sacred madman, and
prophet.

To be sure, the twentieth century saw something of a rehabilitation of pre-Pushkinian poetry, with such important figures as Marina Tsvetaeva, Osip Mandelstam, and later Joseph Brodsky, inspired by the stubborn obscurity and exhilarating harshness of Derzhavin. But the Modernist emphasis on the pursuit of originality was not congenial to an understanding of the deliberate conventionalism of eighteenth-century writing. Typical was Vladimir Nabokov, whose commentary on *Evgeny Onegin* lambasted the insipidity of Karamzin and the unreadable dreariness of the epic poet Mikhail Kheraskov, and unwillingly allowed to Derzhavin only 'touches of rough genius'. In poetry, the voice employed by Pushkin in his writings about the poet, allying ironical scepticism to a defiant assertion of the value of inspiration, became the definitive means of conveying artistic experience. The 1910s and 1920s saw a revival of 'Pushkinian' devices in prose too – the use of frame narratives, epigraphs, texts-within-texts, and other strategies marking the distance of a tale from reality, its contingency upon style rather than observation.

Despite the gesticulation on the part of writers towards Pushkin in terms of theme, and the borrowing of vocabulary and of forms with a 'Pushkinian' resonance, the work of later generations was by no means constrained by what Pushkin had done. Those genres in which Pushkin did not work were often to prove more productive than those in which he did. Though Andrey Sinyavsky described Pushkin's poetry as 'filled with a mass of personal material', the amount of strictly 'personal material' in Pushkin's lyric poetry, as opposed to his letters or notebook jottings, is actually rather limited, and this material always appears in transmuted form. Apparently confessional poems, written in the first person, are in fact 'costumed confessions' – that is, spoken in the words of some invented character. And the 'costumes' that Pushkin chose to put on, both in his lyric verse and in his drama and fiction, were bewilderingly varied. Pushkin's essays and jottings make it clear that he was temperamentally akin both to Mozart and Salieri, the apparently antithetical heroes of one of his *Little Tragedies*;

Hermann, the dogged, neurotic German protagonist of *The Queen of Spades*, and the effortlessly charming Tomsky, a prattling gossip from high society, are both authorial alter egos. Though the mode of 'costumed confession' is characteristic of Russian literature (it is found, for instance, in Lermontov's *Hero of our Time*, or in Akhmatova's early poetry), the sheer range of masks that Pushkin adopted was unique.

Nor was confessional poetry the only genre that was not anticipated in Pushkin's work. As Lidiya Ginzburg argued in a classic history of nineteenth-century Russian literature, *On Psychological Prose*, it was Aleksandr Herzen, in *My Past and Thoughts*, who pioneered the genre of confessional prose, employing a searingly emotional rhetoric that would probably have embarrassed Pushkin. Conversely, Pushkin's wonderfully vivid, playful, and self-deprecating letters have few successors in Russian tradition. Later masters of the epistolary form, such as Marina Tsvetaeva, inclined to literary-philosophical abstraction and to lamentation on the unfairness of fate rather than to concrete detail and teasing humour. So far as the theatre was concerned, Pushkin wrote no dramatic comedies, which both before and after his lifetime constituted the glory of the Russian theatre. (Gogol's *The Government Inspector*, ensconced in the international repertory as a unique masterpiece, was the successor to eighteenth-century texts such as Fonvizin's *The Minor* or Knyazhnin's *The Boaster*, and the inspiration for Aleksandr Ostrovsky, the prolific mainstay of the mid-nineteenth-century Russian theatre.) Nor did Pushkin contribute to the extremely important genre of tragicomedy, as exemplified in Chekhov's *The Cherry Orchard* or Mayakovsky's *The Bed-Bug*. His greatest achievements remained splendidly isolated. To be sure, *Evgeny Onegin* inspired imitations, but none of these were more than entertaining exercises in light verse. The psychological complexity of *Boris Godunov* was captured in Musorgsky's operatic setting of the play, rather than in Aleksey Konstantinovich Tolstoy's trilogy of historical dramas about Boris, his predecessors and his successors, works of a painstaking dullness rather than the young Pushkin's sketchy brilliance.

If Pushkin can be seen as a pioneer, it is of 'mixed genre' texts. The narrative poem with prose 'frame' in *The Egyptian Nights* (1835) was, for instance, paralleled (though not imitated) in Karolina Pavlova's *A Double Life* (1844–7), a prose story using poetry to represent the thoughts and dreams of its protagonist, Cecilia. But given the preoccupation of Romantic literature throughout Europe with new and hybrid forms (take Heine's 'verse novel' *Atta Troll*, or the use of song to represent Mignon's imaginative world in Goethe's *Wilhelm Meister*) it is difficult to argue that the intergeneric text in Russian literature derives wholly from Pushkin's influence.

Even the conventional view of Pushkin's centrality to the Russian literary language can only be partly endorsed. Much of Pushkin's streamlining of syntax had been anticipated in the eighteenth century, not only in the writings of Nikolay Karamzin, traditionally seen as the pre-Pushkinian pioneer, but also in humbler sources, such as the memoirs of Princess Natalya Dolgorukaya, produced in 1767 as a private chronicle for her descendants, and in translations from the French of novels and of conduct books. Besides, as the scholar Boris Gasparov, among others, has argued, the Pushkinian/Karamzinian line was only one of many literary orientations in the early nineteenth century; other writers were as likely to react against it as they were to espouse it.

So far as prose fiction went, Pushkin's heritage was similarly idiosyncratic. A sore point for advocates of Pushkin's role as the 'founding father of Russian literature' has been the writer's failure, among his many brilliant excursions into diverse genres, to provide models for the enormous psychological novels that have, since the late nineteenth century, been internationally regarded as Russia's greatest contribution to world literature. Even so determinedly individual a

13. Ostrovsky, *Too Clever By Half.*

Ostrovsky's *Too Clever By Half* (1868) in an 'eccentric' circus staging by the film director Sergey Eisenstein (1923): a dozen or so ginger-haired clowns cavort provocatively on a climbing-frame set. Ostrovsky, the linchpin of the Russian theatre in the mid-nineteenth century, is a clear case of a successful writer whose work bears little or no relation to Pushkin's (with the possible exception of his fairy-tale drama *The Snow Maiden*). Unlike Pushkin, he was a professional man of the theatre, many of whose plays, so far from being brilliant but theatrically problematic experiments, were competent formulaic comedies lifted above the rut by the author's extraordinary ear for vulgar speech, vivid sense of the ridiculous, and infectious misanthropy. *The Storm*, on the other hand, was a full-blooded melodrama of merchant life that was quite out of kilter with Pushkin's emotional delicacy. Which is not to belittle Ostrovsky's achievements as a dramatist: his plays have a firm place on the international stage (*The Storm* inspired Janáček's opera *Katerina Kabanova*, for instance), as well as the national one. And in early twentieth-century Russia, their familiarity bred not contempt but daring on the part of directors, including Meyerhold and Stanislavsky, as well as Eisenstein.

Modernist as Nabokov, who held much Russian Realist prose to be as bogus in intention as it was garrulous in expression, and who detested psychological literalism, commented of Pushkin's Evgeny Onegin that he is 'fluid and flaccid as soon as he starts to feel, as soon as he departs from the existence he has acquired from his maker in terms of colorful parody and as a catchall for many irrelevant and immortal matters'. It was above all as a triumph of surface-painting that he admired the novel. To be sure, *Evgeny Onegin* is stylistically diverse and has a narrator who plays many parts (a friend of the characters, a mouthpiece for

them, an ironic commentator upon folly, a sympathizer in time of grief).
Yet even Tatiana remains a symbol rather than a counterfeit of lived
reality, a creature of idealism rather than representation. She is as much
a manifestation of the creative sensibility as a portrait of a provincial
young lady. If her letter to Evgeny, written when awake, is a tissue of
quotations from books she has read, her dream of Evgeny surrounded
by strange creatures is narrated in the language of Pushkin's own lyric
ballads.

None of this has resonance in, say, the writing of Tolstoy, Dostoevsky,
or Chekhov. Pushkin's characters usually do not have their own
voices: they are pegs upon which the fabric of authorial brilliance
is hung (the same is true of Gogol's characters, with the exception
of the Mayor in the *Government Inspector*, who, in his final outburst
of rage against the trick that has been played on him, achieves a
truly personal eloquence unlike anything else in the play). Pushkin's
acidly detached portrayal of Hermann and Liza allows little space to
speech from within the characters: Hermann in particular remains
enigmatic because he is always seen from outside. The furthest
possible point from this was reached in Dostoevsky's extraordinary,
and by both national and international standards revolutionary, story
Notes from Underground, in which we have no point of orientation but
the voice of the central character himself, tormenting us with his
capricious and contradictory statements from the very first sentence
of the novel:

> I am a sick man. A bitter and spiteful man. An unattractive man. I think
> that my liver has something wrong with it. But actually I don't give a stuff
> about being ill and I'm not even sure what's wrong with me. I'm not
> going for treatment and I never have gone for treatment, even though I
> do respect doctors and medicines. And on top of that, I'm superstitious;
> superstitious enough, even, to respect medicine. (I'm educated enough
> not to be superstitious, but I still am superstitious.) No, sir, the reason I
> don't go for treatment is out of spite. You probably won't want to

understand that. Well, I understand you there. But of course I won't
manage to explain to you precisely whose nose I aim to put out of joint
with my spite . . .

No English translation can imitate the grammar of the original, which
employs the flexibility of Russian syntax in order to place the adjective
in a different position in each of the first sentences, so that the cadence
rises to a pitch of hysterical triumph on 'unattractive'. But the nature of
the rhetorical stategies comes across. As a statement is presented, it is
immediately contradicted; just as contradictory is the Underground
Man's combination of insistent solitariness and inability to do without
his listener, the antagonist who 'probably won't want to understand'.
The Underground Man's confession is presented without any of the
devices customarily used to establish a memoir as 'real'. There is no
diary discovered after his death, his listener remains anonymous, and
there is no motivating occasion (in contrast, the murderer in Tolstoy's
Kreutzer Sonata makes his confession in a train carriage, a propos a
discussion of marriage). *Notes from Underground* breached the literary
etiquette of Pushkin's prose as energetically as its monstrously
paranoid, intolerant, and rude narrator poured contempt on the
behaviour conventions of polite society.

To be sure, aspects of Pushkin's prose were to be treated as exemplary
by some later writers. For Chekhov, it was Pushkin's sparing use of
figurative language, his preference for metonyms over metaphors, that
was particularly attractive. For Tolstoy, it was above all the directness
and immediacy of Pushkin's opening paragraphs that had weight. The
second sentence of *Anna Karenina* – 'Everything had got mixed up in
the Oblonsky household' – has the deliberate flatness of the first line
of *The Queen of Spades*, 'A game of cards was going on one day in the
residence of Narumov, an officer in the horse guards.'

Yet Tolstoy, the most 'Pushkinian' of writers in terms of his way of
beginning a narrative, was decidedly anti-Pushkinian in other respects.

The caricatured Napoleon in *War and Peace* is at the far end of the representational spectrum from Pushkin's ambivalent, but fervent, tributes to the leader's Romantic grandeur. 'Napoleon' (1822) opens with lines that employ the cosmic imagery of the eighteenth-century formal ode to evoke the French emperor's transcendent greatness:

> The fateful destiny is played out:
> The great man has flickered into darkness.
> In gloomy unfreedom has rolled to an end
> The thunderous age of Napoleon.

For Tolstoy in *War and Peace*, 'providence' replaced 'destiny', and characters achieved greatness in the sight of their God and of their literary creator because of their lack of aspiration to the 'greatness' represented here. In Pushkin's writings, for instance *The Bronze Horseman*, the word 'idol' occupied a vital place, capturing an ambiguous configuration of greatness and moral transgression. In Tolstoy's mind, all idols, by definition, could only deceive, and in attempting to escape their common humanity were certain to reveal their tawdry and hollow true selves. The fact that Tolstoy's father, a member of Pushkin's own generation, had made him learn 'Napoleon' by heart in the nursery did everything other than ensure piety towards Pushkin and his hero.

Compared with Pushkin's sense that prose should be 'modest' and 'lucid', too, the expansiveness of Tolstoy's vast 'baggy monsters' was provocative to the point of impertinence. The epilogue of *The Queen of Spades* ties up the ends with exaggerated neatness, underlining the fact that this is a piece of fiction. Tolstoy's endings, on the other hand, are made fuzzy by their epilogues and afterwords. There is the sense of the writer returning again and again to subjects he could not bear to abandon. And the intimations of fate that play an ambiguous role in *The Queen of Spades* were, for Tolstoy, always escapable. If there is some sense that Hermann may really have been taken to the Countess's house by an 'unknown power', a malign supernatural force, albeit one within him, a character's belief that his or her fate was 'foreshadowed' was, for Tolstoy, an indication of psychic morbidity, of a bent to self-destruction.

Tolstoy, then, was an example of a reader who read Pushkin 'like a poet' – a term which Pushkin himself understood to mean a creative personality in a broad sense, someone who might be inspired tangentially, rather than literally, by what he or she read.

It took a century or so after *War and Peace* was published before any writer repudiated Pushkin as boldly, but also as creatively, as Tolstoy had. But by the 1960s, decades of force-fed patriotism had inspired – at least among some unofficial Soviet writers – a marked disaffection with the literary classics. Varlam Shalamov, for example, began one of his *Kolyma Tales* with a bitter parody of the first line of *The Queen of Spades*: 'One day they were playing cards in the barracks residence of Naumov, one of the guards of the horses in the prison camp.' The irrelevance of the original to Soviet life is cruelly underlined. A more extended repudiation of Pushkin was to be found in the poetry of Joseph Brodsky, whose personal canon of great Russian poets (Derzhavin, Baratynsky, Mandelstam) demonstratively side-stepped 'the father of Russian literature'.

Brodsky's important sequence, 'Twenty Sonnets for Maria Stuart' (1974), for example, distances itself from Pushkin in a variety of ways, overt and hidden. It selects a verse form (the sonnet) which Pushkin scarcely employed. Alliteration, which is a striking device throughout the cycle, is used far more obviously than in Pushkin's works. Brodsky also makes clear from the outset that the 'muse' to whom 'Maria Stuart' is addressed is a fantasy, an invention, something that will 'step down from the screen/and enliven the parks like a statue' (sonnet no. 1). The addressee is both less and more real than the statues to which several of Pushkin's late poems are addressed (and which are evoked in Brodsky's simile). She is an emanation of a film that the lyric hero saw as a boy, where 'Sarah/Leander walked click-click to the scaffold' (sonnet no. 2). That is, she is an artistic vision of a kind far less substantial than a sculpture. Yet at the same time, the cycle insists on her actual, physical existence, as someone who is the object of a desire deserving consummation, so that 'Scotland becomes our mattress' (sonnet no. 8). And to mark his distance still further, Brodsky continually, and, from the point of view of conventional literary piety, impertinently, quotes from Pushkin's love poems in order to undermine their emotional rhetoric, most particularly through glaring lexical dislocations that are utterly contrary to the spirit of Pushkin's harmonious combinations of disparate poetic styles. A case in point is the wry parody, in the sixth sonnet, of Pushkin's 'I loved you' (translated here by Peter France):

> *I loved you. And my love (or maybe*
> *it's only pain) still stabs me through the brain.*
> The whole thing's shattered into smithereens.
> I tried to shoot myself – using a gun
> isn't so simple. And the temples: which one,
> the right or left? Reflection, not the shakes,
> kept me from acting. Jesus! what a mess!
> *I loved you with such strength, such hopelessness*
> *may God send you in others* – not a chance!
> He may be capable of many things,
> but – with Parmenides – won't reinspire
> the fire in the blood, the bones' crunching collapse,
> swelling the lead in fillings with desire
> to touch – 'your hips', I must delete – your lips.

Apart from the two direct quotations from Pushkin (italicized here – for the full text of the original poem, see Chapter 6), the poem's parodistic relationship to its original is established by the use, in line 12 of the Russian, of the archaic article *sei* – 'yonder fire' would be correct in terms of register. But the original is used as a mere backing canvas for purely Brodskian (and twentieth-century) rhetorical embroidery. This includes the vulgarism *byust* ('bust', here rendered 'hips') in line 14 (Pushkin would have used the high-style *persi*, or 'breasts', in the context of a love poem), the reference to 'the shakes' in line 6, the throwaway mention of Parmenides (the fifth-century Greek rationalist philosopher who held that only what exists can be known) in line 11, and, especially, the ironic undermining of the allusion to God in line 9.

Such a direct, defiant repudiation of Pushkin qua Pushkin, based upon a thorough knowledge of his works, remained a rarity even in twentieth-century Russian literature. Far more common was the attempt to find an 'alternative' Pushkin to the 'father of Russian literature' or 'Soviet patriot before his time' by looking once more to Pushkin's own works. Just as censorship fostered 'Aesopian language', so did the narrow, official image of 'the greatest Russian writer' foster an 'Aesopian Pushkin'. From the mid-1930s, writing about Pushkin, a self-evidently 'safe' topic (unlike the late Dostoevsky, with his notorious loathing for the Russian revolutionary movement and devotion to the Orthodox Church), could allow writers to voice issues that would have been utterly taboo if touched upon directly.

A case in point was Anna Akhmatova's essays on Pushkin. These emphasized Pushkin's talent for 'encryption' – at a point when Akhmatova herself was evolving a protective obscurity in response to institutionalized oppression. Equally, Akhmatova's emphasis on Pushkin's struggle for dignity in a world reduced to moral squalor by authoritarianism articulated her view of the position of the Soviet writer. Exactly so did Shostakovich use citations from his own setting of Pushkin's poem 'The barbarian painter with his somnolent brush' in order to weave the theme of posthumous artistic justification into his Fifth Symphony, his first major public work after the vicious vilification that had greeted *Lady Macbeth of Mtsensk* in 1936.

To be sure, the emphasis here on the writer's sacred role made these unofficial views of Pushkin close to official views, in terms of tone if not interpretation. But there were also other, less solemn, 'alternative Pushkins'. Many preferred, in the words of Andrey Sinyavsky, to approach Pushkin 'not by the grand front entrance lined with busts wearing expressions of unrelenting nobility on their faces, but with the help of the anecdotes and caricatures that have been dreamed up by street culture as a kind of response to, revenge for, Pushkin's resounding fame'. To continue Sinyavsky's own metaphor, writers approached Pushkin by the back door or 'black entrance' rather than the front or 'parade' one.

The smutty tone of the phrase 'back door' pointed to the fact that intimacy in all its forms was a governing trope of twentieth-century anti-establishment literature, which also led to an emphasis on Pushkin's clandestine writings. The *Gabrieliad*, an irreverent romp depicting the insemination of the Virgin Mary by Satan and the Angel Gabriel as well as God, which had circulated in manuscript during Pushkin's lifetime and been published in full only after the Revolution, now attained canonical status. Preparation for the first 'complete' edition of Pushkin in the 1920s turned up quantities of private correspondence, rough drafts, jottings, and so on, which were equally helpful to the construction of a new, 'intimate' Pushkin. Most obviously, they explored subject matter uncongenial to the decorous image of a 'national poet'. Here, Pushkin could be found boasting of having wiped his 'sinful hole' with pages torn from the prolific occasional poet Count Khvostov's latest book, or comparing the 'colon and comma' that ornamented his loins with the mere 'comma' of a politically powerful, but sexually disadvantaged, grandee. But the new Pushkin materials offered more than such glimpses of the forbidden. They also contributed to a growing sense of the writer's manuscript as a text in itself, not just an intermediate stage between inspiration and publication (as Pushkin himself, whatever his concerns about textual integrity, had certainly seen it). After 1928, as censorship became fiercer, and more and more writers practised 'the genre of silence', or composed texts for 'the desk drawer', it was the manuscript that alone held the promise of eluding social control. Books might be purged from libraries, but in the words of Mikhail Bulgakov, whose *Master and Margarita* was one of the most famous manuscripts to survive the Stalin years (though Bulgakov himself did not), 'manuscripts don't burn'. What was more, with their doodled landscapes, portraits of salon beauties, ducks, devils, and chargers, Pushkin's manuscripts had a liveliness, a physical presence ('facture') that had characterized the avant-garde publications of the 1910s and 1920s, but which began to disappear as control over print culture tightened in the 1930s. (Ill. 9.)

As Pushkin's negligently scrawled self-portraits presented a welcome alternative view of the poet to the congealed bronze of statues, so, for 1960s Modernists, it was precisely the poet's immateriality, his 'emptiness', his 'chatter', his amoralistic and slippery variability of style, his idiosyncratic undefinability, that appealed. There was a revival of interest in Pushkin as parodist, an identity that had also appealed to writers in the 1920s, when even the sacred notion of the poet as prophet had been subject to ironic appropriation (the writer Vikenty Veresaev had wondered in 1929 whether 'Monument', like the character of Evgeny Onegin, might not be a sardonic travesty of Romantic stereotype: 'Is this poem maybe not just a parody?'). Soviet Socialist Realists had seen themselves, in all seriousness, as heirs to Tolstoy and Turgenev, and pontificated solemnly to readers about their approach to the 'writer's craft'. Underground or semi-official writers of the 1960s and 1970s, on the other hand, preferred to approach classic works of Russian literature via the 'back door' of irony. Venedikt Erofeev's *Moscow-Petushki* was a *reductio ad absurdum* of the official practice of using citations from the classics as a way of displaying a text's cultural credentials – texts from the Bible to the labels of tins of boot-polish appeared in a disorderly profusion, with no sense of relative importance. And in Dmitry Prigov's mock-obituary in the style of *Pravda*, Pushkin's essential frivolity was used to undermine the pomposity of official biography and of recognized writers:

The Central Committee of the Communist Party of the Soviet Union, the Supreme Soviet of the USSR, and the Soviet Government announce with the very deepest regret that on the 10 February (29 January, Old Style) 1837, as the result of a tragic duel, the course of the life of the great Russian poet Aleksandr Sergeevich Pushkin, aged 37, has come to a sudden and untimely end.

Comrade Pushkin was always distinguished by high principles, a sense of responsibility, and a demanding attitude towards himself and others. In every post that he was deputed to occupy he displayed boundless fidelity to the appointed task, a military valour and heroism, and all the elevated qualities of a patriot, a citizen, and a poet.

He will always remain in the hearts of his friends and those who knew him well as a rake, a joker, a tearaway, and a terrible boozer.

Pushkin's name will live for ever in the memory of the Russian people as the eternal flame of Russian poetry.

From 'the father of Russian literature', Pushkin had become a jester, a participant at bachelor revels. He was even paid the dubious compliment of a pornographic forgery, his so-called Secret Memoirs of 1836 and 1837, which confessed, among other things, to three-in-a-bed frolics with his wife Natalya and her sister Aleksandra. And his key works now included, besides *Evgeny Onegin* (not as Belinsky's 'encyclopedia of Russian life', but as a playful piece of eavesdropping on gossip and an example of 'manipulation of plot'), *The Little House at Kolomna*, *The Gabrieliad*, and *Count Nulin*.

Chapter 5
'Awakening noble feelings with my lyre'
Writers as 'masters of minds'

A literary sermon is freer and more independent than a treatise; it often looks above real phenomena, far beyond them, sketching out its prophetic words on the distant and empty horizon.

(Pavel Annenkov, 1858)

In the last chapter, we saw how the pomposity of the Pushkin cult provoked an understanding of Pushkin as jester, as *homo ludens*, a pleasant acquaintance to be 'strolled' with, rather than as a disdainful and frowning pedagogue. Pushkin became the herald of meaning as non-meaning, the poet above all of *The Little House of Kolomna* (1830), which concludes its bizarre and studiedly pointless saga of a transvestite cook with the following words:

Here's a moral for you: in my view
It's risky to hire a cook for free;
For a person born a man to dress up
In skirts, is curious and has no point;
After all, sooner or later he will be forced
To give himself a shave, which doesn't quite agree
With a lady's nature . . . But that's the very most
That you'll squeeze out of this slight tale.

But frivolity of this kind is not the key to Pushkin's entire output. Equally characteristic of him was the didactic view of literature expressed in 'Monument' – that a writer was responsible for 'awakening the noble feelings' of an entire nation. Even the ending of *The Little House at Kolomna* had a lesson to teach – that literature did not have to be taken seriously. It sprang from Pushkin's frustration with Russian readers' obsession with morals and messages, as powerfully expressed in 'The Poet and the Crowd' (1828), a rebuke to those who, on hearing a 'song', were capable only of responding with stupid questions:

> What is he strumming about? what is he teaching us?
> Why is he exciting and tormenting hearts
> Like a capricious wizard?
> His song is free as the wind,
> But also fruitless as the wind:
> What is the use of it to us?

And in *The Queen of Spades* (1834), any moralizing ambitions that might have been expected in a tale of compulsive gambling are undercut because story-telling and writing are shown within the story itself as frivolous, unreliable, deceptive, no more than 'chatter to spin out a mazurka'.

But moral commentary is not avoided altogether. When Hermann appears in Liza's room to undeceive her about the reasons behind his long-distance courtship (he has in fact been writing her passionate letters so he can inveigle himself inside the house to confront her guardian, the Countess), the narrator observes: 'She wept bitterly, seized by belated and painful repentance.' Had Pushkin opted for moral neutrality, he could have used a different phrase (for example, 'seized by sudden, painful understanding'). But the narrator is made to espouse Christian moral vocabulary ('repentance'), and the adjective 'belated' passes explicit judgement (Liza's feelings are appropriate, but she has ignored the voice of conscience too long). Equally, there is no doubt that the duel between Evgeny Onegin and Lensky is to be understood as a form of homicide licensed by civilization, though this point is conveyed indirectly, through a comically embittered disquisition upon the joys of revenge:

> It is pleasant to enrage an obtuse enemy
> With an impudent epigram [. . .]
> Pleasanter if he, my friends,
> Bawls out in stupid rage: 'That's me!'
> Still pleasanter to prepare in silence
> An honourable grave for him,
> And to shoot silently at his pale forehead
> From a well-bred distance;
> But sending him to the land of his fathers
> Is unlikely to be a pleasant experience.

It would be absurd to interpret the final proposition here as a stylistic mannerism, introduced merely in order to puncture the overblown rhetoric of revenge with plain speaking. But wry humour pushes just out of reach an obvious truth – that killing even one's enemies is not nice.

Delicate irony of this kind, though, rests on a fragile pyramid of assumptions about the way that readers are likely to react. As Yury Lotman has pointed out, in Pushkin's generation the duel was well on its way to being regarded as 'ritual murder' (and less melodramatically, as a form of posturing that was fatuous in adult males, an interpretation that hovers at the fringes of Pechorin's duel with his charlatan-double Grushnitsky in Lermontov's *The Hero of Our Time* (1841), and came fully into its own in Chekhov's representations of duelling half a century later). In a society where the duel was universally accepted as the central means of settling affairs of honour, an assault upon the practice of duelling as immoral would have needed to be expressed more explicitly. In the eighteenth and early nineteenth centuries, Russian writers had a strong sense that readers of serious literature (as opposed to fortune-telling books or church calendars) belonged to a unified group, even if some had a less sophisticated understanding of literature than others, and needed to be reminded of certain elementary critical truths – that literature was not the same thing as life, and that a narrator should not necessarily be identified with the author. This sense of integration resulted, in the main, from the fact that the educated population was so small.

In the 1830s and 1840s, as intellectual life expanded to include a much broader range of social groups, in particular ambitious male provincials from the middle ranks of Russian society, the notion of educated consensus began to break down. The first symptom was factionalism within the literary world, particularly squabbling between patrician writers such as Pushkin, and literary journalists, most notorious among whom was the arch-conservative, police spy, editor of *The Northern Bee*, and popular novelist Faddey Bulgarin. Once the sense that all educated people belonged to the same circle had disintegrated, so too did the expectation that moral values were shared and could be taken for granted. This created a pressure for the expression of consensus within a text by means of overt commentary and explication; for the frank didacticism that had been the source of irony in literary texts since the end of the eighteenth century.

Hence, of many possible Pushkins that Pushkin himself had created, it was the writer as 'master of minds', and teacher to his nation, that carried most weight among his contemporaries and immediate successors. In 1834, Belinsky sought to prescribe to Pushkin the ways in which he should work, complaining that the writer had moved from *Poltava* and *Boris Godunov* (shorthand for 'works of unassailable seriousness and national importance') to 'empty, lifeless fairy-tales' (it is a shock to realize that Belinsky had in mind Pushkin's brilliant condensation of Shakespeare's *Measure for Measure*, *Angelo*). And the transition from a view of the writer as metatextual ironist to an emphasis upon responsibility to society can clearly be seen in the case of Nikolay Gogol. Gogol's story *The Nose* (1836) had poked fun at the idea of morally improving literature: the tale ended not with a moral, but with the narrator sputtering into silence as he tried to explain what meaning there could possibly be in an anecdote about Major Kovalyov's lost nose reincarnated as a senior civil servant. But a decade later, Gogol had developed a very different notion of the writer's vocation. In his notorious treatise, *Selected Passages From Correspondence with Friends* (1847), he claimed that Pushkin had been the only reader of *Dead Souls* to understand the high moral purpose of the novel, and asserted: 'A writer's duty is not only to provide pleasant amusement for the mind and the taste; he will pay dearly if his works do not disseminate something of use to the soul and if they convey no moral instruction to their readers.' While a great many of Gogol's opinions in *Selected Passages* were attacked by both radicals and conservatives (not many people were impressed by Gogol's suggestion that the landowner should burn banknotes in front of his peasants in order to teach them indifference to money), his emphasis on the writer's duty to convey 'moral instruction' was not challenged. Rather, the central point in criticism of *Selected Passages*, as voiced, for example, in a famous open letter written by Belinsky to Gogol in 1847, was that Gogol had betrayed the writer's duty to be a moral instructor by imparting the wrong sort of message. Radicals and conservatives alike now valued literature on the grounds of its *ideinost'*, or confrontation of important topical issues.

To be sure, *ideinost'* did not reign unchallenged after 1840. The conviction among politically committed critics that realist fiction, or indeed journalistic reportage, were superior to lyric poetry provoked the authors of verse into questioning utilitarian theories of literature. (A notable case in point was Apollon Grigoriev, a Moscow critic, author of 'gypsy romances', and vehement enemy of Belinsky, Nekrasov, and Dobrolyubov, as well as one of many Russian writers to have been a drinker on an epic scale.) In the late nineteenth century, the Russian

Decadents followed their French counterparts in insisting upon the autonomy of art, and in maintaining a cult of self-interest (the ideal Decadent hero or heroine, rather than committing him- or herself to the improvement of society, was dedicated to the pursuit of pleasure and sensual gratification alone).

But the desire to separate art from moral or political issues remained a marginal phenomenon, as was illustrated when Tolstoy, the towering figure of the late nineteenth century and a commentator respected and feared by figures belonging to every political grouping, lent his immense authority to an attack on the Decadent cult of beauty. *What is Art?* (1898) set out a sustained and powerful case against the aesthetic understanding of art, which was to be valued, in Tolstoy's view, for its sincere expression of feeling and for its commitment to the cause of good. The pervasiveness of populism in the Russian intelligentsia, and of the view that the duty of educated people was to help the so-called 'grey masses', meant that attempts to fuse art and politics were more common than attempts to separate the two, even among the 'Decadents' whom Tolstoy had attacked. For a while in 1906–7, the short-lived 'Mystical Anarchist' movement was the expression of a drive to unite Modernist literature, religious philosophy, and socialism; after 1917, a number of Modernist writers became ardent supporters of Bolshevism and participants in its newly fledged cultural institutions. The Symbolist poet Valery Bryusov, for example, was made responsible for setting up training schemes for Soviet writers; Mayakovsky and other left avant-gardists churned out jingles and posters for the Rosta (Russian Telegraph Agency) windows in Moscow.

But there were also less obvious ways in which art and politics impacted upon each other. Marina Tsvetaeva, whose fierce independence from any party line was to make her deeply unpopular both in post-revolutionary Moscow and after her emigration to Prague and later to Paris, and who was one of the most formidably gifted

Modernist poets, became embroiled, after 1917, in one crusade after another. Her magnificent tribute to the 'White', anti-Soviet forces in the Russian Civil War, *The Swan's Demesne* (1921), written in Soviet Moscow, was followed by an equally controversial tribute to Mayakovsky, 'the draught-horse angel', published in Berlin in 1923, a year after Tsvetaeva's emigration to the West.

The acceptance among many Russian writers that art and ethics were compatible was in part a result of the ambitions of governments, both before and after the Revolution, to regulate morality and the arts. There was generally an inverse relationship between the severity of censorship and the production of studiedly amoral or self-consciously frivolous works of art: it is a rare writer who will risk his or her life or freedom for the sake of a joke. In any case, the Western liberal construct of a 'civic sphere', according to which cultural institutions, along with education and regulation of the urban environment, are assumed to be in signal respects autonomous and 'above politics', did not necessarily have a greater hold on the minds of writers hostile to Tsarist and Soviet power than it did upon political leaders themselves. At some periods in nineteenth-century Russian history, 'democratic censorship' (that is, the drive of Russian radical critics and editors to coerce authors into political conformity) was, as a recent historian has commented, 'as much a force to be reckoned with as the official variety'.

All of this means that it is a serious mistake to argue that 'classic Russian literature [. . .] is rarely overtly didactic' (to quote a Western historian of Russia). On the contrary, 'overt didacticism' was one of classic Russian writers' great strengths. Only a deliberately wayward reader could fail to recognize that Saltykov-Shchedrin's *The Golovlyov Family* was an eloquent denunciation of the moral bankruptcy of the serf-owning class, or that his *History of a Town* was a vicious satire on autocratic rule. The point was not that Russian writers avoided sermons and exemplary tales, but that they narrated these with extraordinary rhetorical force.

Yet the creepy Yudushka Golovlyov in the first novel and the stentorian Mayor Ugryum-Burcheev in the second were more than simply vehicles for Saltykov's ideological points. It was literary critics, rather than authors, who relentlessly classified characters in terms of their supposed expression of contemporary ills, effacing the differences between Evgeny Onegin, Pechorin, and Andrey Bolkonsky so they could be rounded up into a shorn herd of 'superfluous men'. In similar vein, Nikolay Dobrolyubov's essay on Goncharov's novel *Oblomov*, 'What is Oblomovitis?', presented the book as a parable about idleness versus industriousness, ignoring the fact that the superlatively indolent and gluttonous Oblomov had stimulated his creator's fancy as the book's positive hero, self-righteous Stolz, had not.

For writers, as opposed to commentators, there was always a tension between ideological and imaginative aims. The frequent practice among writers of composing prefaces, afterwords, and commentaries upon their own literary texts was a manifestation of the 'intergeneric' character of Russian literature, its desire to bridge the gap between fiction and non-fiction (note the pasting of real documents into Tolstoy's *War and Peace*). But it also pointed to an awareness that literary convention interfered with the straightforward communication of messages.

A striking instance of the clash between fiction and ideology was Tolstoy's late story *The Kreutzer Sonata* (1889). An 'Afterword' written by Tolstoy after the book was published endorsed the outrageous case made by the central character, Pozdnyshev: it insisted that absolute celibacy was the only morally acceptable form of human existence. Tolstoy also expressed consternation that readers should have found it so hard to grasp the point of his story. But Pozdnyshev, who was shown in the opening sections of the story itself swarming with nervous tics and feeding his caffeine addiction with glass after glass of the strongest tea, was hardly the best advocate of views that his creator (then energetically recommending abstention from intoxicating substances) apparently wished to be taken seriously. The character did not even have the grace to repent his misdeeds or sympathize with his victim. It was and is difficult to see the story as a fable; it is much easier to appreciate it as a grim and convincing sketch of the mentality of a murderer, prowling in his stocking feet through his own house to surprise his victim, and detachedly remembering the feeling of his knife cutting through first whalebone, then flesh. A similar communicative uncertainty was evident in *Anna Karenina*, which was at once a moral tale about appropriate married life and a delineation of the horrors of that life. Exploiting marriage as a convenient starting point for an encyclopaedic exploration of Russian society in which *everything* has meaning, it was at the same time obsessed with quotidian detail whose beauty lay in the fact that it had *no* meaning.

But what Mikhail Bakhtin was to term, in a famous study of Dostoevsky, the 'polyphony' of novelistic discourse, the absence in it of a unified, reliable, omniscient point of view, did not necessarily equate with an absence of moral or philosophical certainty. The exuberant linguistic vitality of Gogol's play *The Government Inspector*, which shows the full bawdy energy of colloquial Russian constantly bubbling up through the characters' pathetic attempts to 'speak proper', was intimately related to Gogol's concept of the play as a spiritual morality drama, an illustration of the vices that he believed polluted the human soul and would come to light at the Day of Judgement. For Gogol, linguistic propriety and impropriety were different aspects of the same human error: the assumption that it was possible to conceal frailty and weakness from the all-seeing eye of the deity.

This inextricable blending of 'medium' and 'message', of didactic purpose and expressive range, continued to be found in some Soviet writing, despite an upsurge of state interference on the one hand and intellectual conformity on the other. A case in point was the poetry of Mayakovsky. Mayakovsky's post-1917 writings are often considered to represent a sad falling-off from his early achievements: the writer stands accused of 'stepping on the throat of his own song' (a phrase that he himself uses in his great unfinished testament, 'At the Top of My Voice'). But rather than a historical aberration, a by-way of literary history, the later Mayakovsky was a typical case of a Russian writer in whose work didacticism and art were inseparable. His gripping poem 'Two Not Wholly Usual Occurrences' (1922), for example, juxtaposes scenes of starvation in a Moscow street to a vignette of a 'feast in time of plague' going on at a restaurant, where writers and other intellectuals indulge themselves on the nearest things to delicacies that the crisis-ridden city can provide. Summed up in these bald terms, the piece sounds as crude and obvious as a 'before and after' poster for shampoo, or as an item of anti-capitalist agitprop (the scrawny waif, the bulbous banker) from a 1920s demonstration. But the summary elides the eerie intensity of Mayakovsky's description of the silent Moscow streets, and the shock effect of his opening image, a miscegenated monster, a man-horse:

> Suddenly
> I see
> between me and the window
> a stick-man move.
> Staggering and sliding.
> The stick-man has a horse's head.
> Onward he – it, slides.
> Into its own nostrils it has stuck
> its own fingers:
> three fingers, maybe two.
> Flies squat round the open eyes.
> From the side of its neck
> hangs a vein,
> scattering drops on the streets
> that freeze blackly where they ooze.
> I look and look at the crawling shade:
> shuddering from an unbearable certainty:

> this half-man, half-beast
> must be a figment of my mind.

Safe rationality is soon re-established, and the 'half-man, half-horse' stripped of its mythological significance to be revealed as the head of a starved nag sawn off its scraggy neck by the pen-knife of a desperate Muscovite. Yet the vision, like the nightmare that it resembles, cannot be reduced to an emanation of the everyday: it is not even simply an intimation of death. It remains irreducible, a manifestation of fears normally banished from the modern city, but rising up unsuppressibly at times of extremity.

'Two Not Wholly Usual Occurrences', then, is not an example of imaginative power sacrificed to didactic aims, but of the former and the latter inextricably entwined with each other. It appeals to a sensibility nurtured on psychoanalytical interpretations of myths as archetypes of human experience as much as it no doubt did to a Bolshevik believer convinced that the suffering of the revolutionary years could only be averted through Communism. The gruesome centaur of the Moscow streets, intended as an exemplum to support Mayakovsky's political sermon, is a creature with its own artistic life, perhaps even a metaphor for Modernist poetry as grotesque and unnatural hybrid.

Discussions of Soviet literature's didacticism as aberrant, then, are based on a misapprehension. The ultimate starting point of this is an understandable squeamishness over the nature of the aims that Soviet literature's didactic means had in view. Is it possible to detach artistic value from moral integrity? Can an ode to the Soviet secret police, or to a dictator as vicious as Stalin, ultimately responsible for the death of millions, have any aesthetic value whatever, even when produced by a writer of indisputable artistic talent? These are not merely hypothetical questions. The 'soldiers of Dzerzhinsky' were in fact the subject of a eulogistic poem written by Mayakovsky in 1926. And the mid-1930s, when Socialist Realism was established, also saw the full-scale blossoming of the official cult of Stalin. Writers who wanted to be published needed to manifest *partiinost'*, or fidelity to party values, including (from the late 1930s) the adulation of the leader. In countless poems, stories, and novels, he appeared as the all-seeing friend of every good Soviet citizen:

> Late at night, when every sound falls silent,
> Behind the Kremlin's grey and ancient towers,
> The people of all nations' secret wishes
> Are entrusted to dear Stalin by the world.

This poem by Aleksandr Surkov is terrible by any standards; but writers of real talent also responded to the Stalin cult. An 'Ode to Stalin' by Mandelstam, for instance, is distinguished by its nobility of phrasing and apparent sincerity of feeling.

For many critics belonging to the so-called 'first wave' of the emigration (those who left Russia during or soon after the Revolution), the case against Soviet art was settled in advance. According to Vladislav Khodasevich, a formidable literary critic as well as an outstanding poet: 'Mayakovsky has never been the poet of the revolution, any more than he has ever been a revolutionary poet. His rhetoric is, in fact, the rhetoric of the pogrom, directing violence and invective against anything weak and defenceless, whether that be a German sausage-shop in Moscow or a bourgeois gripped tightly round the throat.' On its own terms, Khodasevich's assessment is hard to assail, but the trouble is that few texts produced in post-1917 Russia would satisfy the criterion of unqualified support for those who suffered under Soviet power. Anna Akhmatova's *Requiem*, a lament for the victims of the Great Purges (the butchery of millions of supposed 'enemies of the people' in 1937–8), and implacably hostile to their torturers, was a work of artistic skill dedicated to a morally impeccable purpose. But this was exceptional. Mostly, the talented writers caught in the different waves of repression dealt in various forms of moral compromise. Bulgakov's novel *The Master and Margarita* (1928–40), for example, juxtaposed to the vision of a corrupt 1920s Moscow, disrupted by Satan, a 'humanized' version of Jesus Christ as socially impotent 'holy fool', moving through a Jerusalem that has uncanny resemblances to the Moscow of the late 1930s. And the novel's epilogue allowed the final word to Woland, Bulgakov's version of Mephisto, who voiced a code of moral relativism in which 'good' and 'evil' were associated with 'light' and 'dark' in the physical world, both being seen as necessary in a life without sensual monotony. For their part, the short stories of Daniil Kharms, such as *Incidents* (1934–6), were brilliant exposures of the dehumanization of life in the 1930s and also texts in which meaningless cruelty itself became a central artistic device, and indeed the object of collusive pleasure for narrator and reader.

In the case of Soviet art, then, it is simply not possible to draw an easy connection between talent and moral steadfastness: many of the most gifted writers had attitudes to tyranny that were equivocal or even admiring. One logical response would be to see nearly everything, including much work produced 'for the desk drawer' (neither Bulgakov nor Kharms had any illusions about being able to publish their later writings), as damnable on the grounds of its ethical dubiety, while consigning *Master and Margarita* to a different circle of hell from, say, Anna Karavaeva's trilogy *The Motherland* (1951), which celebrates the joys of life under the wise governance of the all-seeing Stalin. But this would be to imitate in reverse the narrow-minded cultural politics of the Soviet era, according to which only works imbued with 'Communist morality' and 'progressiveness' deserved to survive (see Chapter 2). It would also conceal the extent to which the moral dilemmas of Soviet artists resembled those of artists at other times and in other socities; as the Russian historian Boris Groys has pointed out, 'historically, art that is universally regarded as good has frequently served to embellish and glorify power'. If one takes a longer or broader view of the tradition of 'embellishing and glorifying power', it is instructive to read Mandelstam's 'Ode to Stalin' in the context of Lomonosov's tributes to Peter I (hardly the most merciful of rulers). It is equally illuminating to compare the Socialist Realist novel with Third Reich fiction, with the Catholic novel of mid-twentieth-century France, Italy, and Ireland, or indeed with formulaic genres such as the 'Harlequin romance' and the detective novel in Britain and America.

A second position is to ignore Soviet art's relationship with political power. If Dostoevsky may be stripped of the Pan-Slavic messianism and anti-Semitism that are painfully obvious in *Diary of a Writer* (1876–81) (and incidentally evident in the novels) and understood as a prophet of universal human freedom, it might be equally legitimate to see the 1920s Mayakovsky as a prophet of liberty in spite of himself. During the final scene in *The Bed-Bug* (1928), the worker Prisypkin, who throughout the play has been relentlessly guyed as a manifestation of the worst kind of petit-bourgeois materialism, suddenly becomes a tragic figure, writhing in a cage to expostulate against the sterile smugness of the Utopian future, and by extension, the stupidity of any community that believes that bringing the future into existence would represent progress.

Alternatively, ethical judgement may be suspended altogether: Soviet literature may be studied in and for itself, and discussed from an 'anthropological' perspective. This means replacing the question of whether the composition of five-year plan novels or odes to Stalin was morally and aesthetically justifiable by the question of what it meant to write them and how they were understood by contemporary readers. Katerina Clark's pioneering study of Socialist Realism, *The Soviet Novel: History as Ritual*, first published in 1981, showed that the homiletic and formulaic novels produced by Socialist Realism were in fact the expressions of powerful myths of self-transformation and loyalty which helped to hold the edgy and unstable new nation of the Soviet Union together. These novels' sketchy characterization and scant consideration for psychological plausibility, and their emphasis on progress by the overcoming of external obstacles, allied them with the devices of traditional Russian folklore on the one hand and classical epic on the other. More recently, other critics, such as David Shepherd, Thomas Lahusen, and Jochen Hellbeck, have analysed the active process of self-shaping undergone by Socialist Realist writers themselves, as they struggled, in private diaries as well as public statements, to mould themselves in the manner required by Party dictates, repeatedly rewriting early versions of their works in order to make them conform with changes in policy. Processes of this kind may not suit Western ideals of artistic and ethical independence, but they were in no sense unambiguous and easy to interpret: one central tragedy of the Stalinist era, indeed, was the amount of complex thought and agonized intelligence that went into producing the simple-minded propaganda novels and poems required by Party policy.

Whichever way, the view of the writer as 'master of minds' was a constant of Russian literature in the nineteenth and twentieth centuries. Even so studiedly ironic a Modernist as Vladimir Nabokov was happy to assert that he was no 'frivolous firebird', but 'a moralist kicking sin, scoffing stupidity, ridiculing the vulgar and cruel – and assigning sovereign power to tenderness, talent, and pride'. Dissent crystallized round the manner in which ethical or aesthetic edification was to be imparted, and the material that it should impart, rather than the question of whether such edification might be tolerated in the first place. The author's right and duty to give such edification was a central plank of Soviet literary culture, in which officially approved authors not only enjoyed material privileges, but were also treated as experts on topical issues of the day. (A typically grotesque example of this was the participation of the prominent Soviet poet Pavel Antokolsky, then in his sixties, in a debate about 'the youth of today' that ran in the Young Communist League newspaper *Komsomol'skaya pravda* during late 1963 and early 1964.) The official view of writers as 'tutors to the masses' did not mean that this role was eschewed by those opposed to the regime. As memoirs and letters make clear, marginal or persecuted writers such as Anna Akhmatova and Joseph Brodsky were credited with peculiar insight into psychological, moral, and aesthetic problems. They were appealed to by intelligent fellow citizens not only as patrons and authoritative readers of literary texts, but as experts on everything from painting, music, architecture, right down to manners, dress, and household decoration.

The fact that regard for writers was so high was one reason why, during the Soviet period, large numbers of Russians became sufferers from 'graphomania', the compulsive desire to spew out writing, and if possible get this into print, irrespective of its merits. Stirred up by 1920s propaganda, which exhorted the Soviet masses to express themselves ('anyone can write!'), graphomania was ubiquitous until the end of Soviet power. It encompassed lyric poems and fiction as well as letters to the press, and avant-garde work as well as official literature. As the émigré writer Svetlana Boym has pointed out, graphomania was 'an embarrassment to literary institutions' of all kinds, unofficial as well as official, since it raised uncomfortable questions about the grounds upon which it was possible to discriminate between the talented and the talentless. Some of the most inventive and interesting novels and stories created under Soviet power were tragi-comic examinations of the fatal affinities between good and bad art. If the genius of Thomas Mann's Aschenbach in 'Death in Venice' has to be taken as a given, and the sensibility of Nabokov's Humbert Humbert at least mimics that of the true artist (though he makes the fatal mistake of confusing fantasy and life), the talents of many Soviet writer-heroes were of a more questionable kind. For example, in Yury Olesha's *Envy* (1927), two different but equally ambiguous writer figures combine genius in perception and invention with social parasitism and paralysis of the will. The pathological fantasist, self-styled inventor, and scribbler of verses-to-order, Ivan Babichev, stands alongside Nikolay Kavalerov, capable of wonderful artistic insights (he sees a bird as a hair-clipper, a scar as a cicatrice from a missing tree-branch) but reduced at the end of the novel to drunken inanition upon the vast, bug-infested, curlicued bedstead of widow Anechka Prokopovich.

The more reflective writers of the 1930s and 1940s, then, were concerned that under a regime which accorded at best a secondary weight to aesthetic criteria in setting down guidelines for publication, all literary production might turn into graphomania. (That such worries were not necessarily chimerical was illustrated by the case of Olesha himself, who sank into alcohol-fuelled despair and the composition of fissiparous fragments during the mid-1930s.) After Stalin's death, though, the term 'graphomania' acquired a different force, as the prize-winning novels of the Stalin era were examined and found wanting, and Socialist Realism itself came under scrutiny. Though the doctrine officially remained in force until 1991, it was irrelevant to a fair amount of the literature published after 1956, even during the relatively repressive 'period of stagnation' (1964–87) which succeeded the 'Khrushchev thaw' of 1954–64. The future of Soviet literature was the subject of heated debates, which occasionally reached journals and public meetings, but were more often carried on over kitchen tables. Those who proclaimed the virtues of artistic autonomy, 'art for art's sake', could point to the many solemn, huge, and forgotten novels that littered the artistic landscape like beached whales. The fact that Solzhenitsyn's novels and stories of the 1950s and early 1960s were preceded by the publication of fulminating articles about parish-pump problems in provincial newspapers, and followed by the composition of yet more polemic, lent fuel to accusations that Solzhenitsyn was a kind of latter-day Pyotr Boborykin or Aleksandr Amfiteatrov (two prolific and long-forgotten late nineteenth-century authors of topical fiction). But it was equally possible for advocates of writing's moral purpose to refer to the cases of the early twentieth-century avant-garde writers Aleksey Kruchonykh and David Burlyuk, whose repetitive output mechanically reproduced futurist devices long after the creative power of these had become exhausted. In Andrey Sinyavsky's 1960 story 'Graphomaniacs', some of the characters were passionately committed to writing in alternative genres – extremely badly; but the story's narrator, Galkin, a 'graphomaniac' of the officially approved kind, and operating a sort of Socialist Realist 'writing by numbers', seemed at least equally ludicrous.

The pessimism expressed in 'Graphomaniacs' was to become a standard theme in post-Thaw discussions of 'the state of Russian literature'. In his 'Catastrophes in the Air', for example, Joseph Brodsky argued that 'politics fills the vacuum left in people's minds and hearts precisely by art', but was just as scathing about avant-garde writing (which, in his view, led to isolation over the vodka bottle) as he was about political commitment. And in 'Soviet Literature: In Memoriam' (1990), Viktor Erofeev took up the theme again, dismissing both dissident and official Soviet writing as of merely local and topical interest.

Fortunately, post-Stalinist literature was considerably more varied and vigorous than such jeremiads proclaimed. To be sure, there were some writers – for example, the novelist and short-story writer Yury Trifonov – in whom the search for a 'middle way' provoked a reversion to a Chekhovian realism of authorial self-effacement plus relentless stress on cultural and moral decline. But a 'prosaics of invisibility' was not the only or even the most favoured interpretation of 'the middle way' among post-Stalinist Russian writers. On the contrary: scepticism about the standing of the writer was (as in the 1920s) matched by an emphasis upon the construction of the art work as a conscious act. This is evident, for example, in Joseph Brodsky's poem elegy 'The Year 1972', which disposed of the figure of 'the poet' in favour of that of 'the wordsmith', working not 'with the aim/of winning fame', but 'for the sake of my native tongue and of writing'. But it was equally clear in the work of writers as committed to the true depiction of real events as Aleksandr Solzhenitsyn and Varlam Shalamov. Though these two writers held very different views about the experience of incarceration in the prison camps (for Solzhenitsyn, the camps opened up vistas of inner freedom and moral renewal; for Shalamov, they were claustrophic 'pits' of moral degradation), they were strikingly similar in terms of the prominence that they gave to the act of writing. The figure of 'walking on fresh snow' at the beginning of Shalamov's huge story cycle *Kolyma Tales* (1978) turned out to be not simply an introduction to camp life, the reader following the prisoners on their journey through the wastes of the far North. It was also a metaphor for the act of writing about untouched material, about retrieving narrative from silence:

> How do you stamp out a path on fresh snow?
> In front walks a man, sweating and swearing, hardly able to move his legs, sinking every minute into the brittle deep snow. [. . .]
> Five or six men follow after, along the narrow and treacherous trail. They walk alongside the track not in it. [. . .]
> Every one of them, no matter how small and weak he is, must stand on a piece of fresh snow, not in someone else's tracks. It's only readers, not writers, who ride on tractors and horses.

If Shalamov drew his readers' attention to the problems of narrative right at the outset of his text, Solzhenitsyn's novels *The First Circle* (1978) and *Cancer Ward*, began, quite traditionally, 'in the middle of things' without preamble. But they too were in literary terms heterogeneous. The citation in *Cancer Ward* of Tolstoy's late story 'What People Live By' (1881), a tale in which an angel comes to live with a poor cobbler and his wife, emphasized that the novel was not merely a representation of a hospital as metaphor for Soviet society, but also a text preoccupied with the miraculous in the mundane (an insight fundamental to understanding the novel's extraordinary last chapter). One of the inset narratives in *The First Circle*, 'Prince Igor', was an illustration of creativity in extremity, a tale told for the joy of the telling, precisely because it did not bear direct or oblique relation to 'real life'. And *One Day in the Life of Ivan Denisovich* (1962), with its refrain, 'How can a well-fed man understand the hungry?' drew attention, like Shalamov's preface to *Kolyma Tales*, to the fact that representing horror was impossible. The more 'true' a narrative, the *less* likely it was to communicate with its anticipated audience. Such utterances were more than merely a rhetorical strategy aimed at shaming the 'well-fed' into attentive silence. They also questioned the function of literature at a time when any utterance might leave only 'the stamp of "good-night" on lips/that could say it to no-one', in the words of a poem from Joseph Brodsky's cycle 'A Part of Speech'.

In the post-Stalin era, then, the concept of writers as 'masters of minds', compromised by Socialist Realism, was the source of serious doubt among many intelligent commentators on, and practitioners of, literature. These included not only Shalamov, recognized by Viktor Erofeev as a 'literary' writer, but also the supposedly 'teleological' Solzhenitsyn. With emerging doubts that the writer's function was or should be purely didactic went a decline in the standing of the novel, the genre most privileged under high Stalinism precisely because of its supposed capacity for weighty moral commentary. (A cartoon published in the humorous magazine *Krokodil* in 1952 showed two writers talking. Writer A to Writer B: 'I've just thought of a great subject for a little short story!'. Writer B: 'Well, get down and write it, then!'. Writer A: 'No, you see the problem is I can't think of how to turn it into a big novel!'.) (Ill. 14.)

However, the compromised standing of moral disquisitions on the one hand, and the novel on the other, was not well understood in the West during the post-Stalin years. Here, many readers looked to Russian writers for the direct and unironic discussion of ethical matters that had become unfashionable in the West after the Second World War. To many commentators in the late 1950s, Boris Pasternak's *Doctor Zhivago* (1957) seemed a much weightier novel than any recent publication in the English language, while Solzhenitsyn's *One Day in the Life of Ivan Denisovich* spoke with an authority recalling Dostoevsky's memoir of prison-camp life *House of the Dead* (1861–2). If Nabokov wished that Tolstoy had exercised his concentration entirely on the free-floating curl hanging down at the back of Anna Karenina's head, many readers, since *Anna Karenina* was published, have been more absorbed by the novel's governing moral themes: whether personal happiness is legitimate at the cost of imposing suffering on others, or whether there may be such a thing as inescapable or deserved suffering. And they have expected

14. Cartoon of two writers by Yu. Gorokhov.

that Tolstoy's successors will provide them with ethical stimulation of just this kind. It was no accident that the first literary award to be supported by Western investors in Russia should have been the Booker Prize for the Russian novel, inspired by the quixotic notion of reviving the genre in the country that many still considered its natural homeland.

Chapter 6
'And don't dispute with fools'
Men, women, and society

> For you, my enchantresses,
>
> Only for you, my beauties . . .
>
> (Pushkin, dedication to *Ruslan and Ludmilla*, 1820)

It would be hard to choose a better example of the difficulties raised by translating Pushkin than the final phrase of 'Monument'. In English, it sounds perfectly banal, like a phrase from a guide to 'making friends and influencing people'. Once again, register plays a part: the Russian word *glupets* has a folksy resonance that would make 'And do not squabble with the daft' in some ways a more adequate rendering. Even so, modern readers are likely to wonder at the combination of apparently incompatible themes in these last two lines. What connection could there be between a dignified command to a poet's muse to 'be obedient to the command of God' and an apparently trivial piece of *savoir vivre*? (To be sure, the phrase bears some relation to a supposed quotation from the Koran jotted down in a draft of *Evgeny Onegin*, 'Don't quarrel with a fool', but since the person citing the quotation was Evgeny himself, and it was preceded with a bare-faced piece of flippancy, 'There's plenty of common sense in the Koran', the sacred text was reduced here to nothing more than a conduct book.)

Yet the rough draft of 'Monument' indicates that 'And don't dispute with fools' was firmly in Pushkin's head from the start of composition. It is the only line in the final three stanzas that was set down straight away in the form that it has in the final text. And the view of the poet as associated not only with the transcendent world of religious and mystical appearance, but also with the banalities of high society, comes up again and again in Pushkin's later poetry. 'The Poet' (1827), for example, is structured round an opposition between 'the concerns of the empty-headed monde' (that is, of high society) and 'the divine word' (that is, of poetic inspiration), an opposition spanned by the poet himself, who lives alternately in each domain. Appealing to the Romantic myth of artists as socially isolated, Pushkin also invokes another and contradictory myth of the artist as *honnête homme*, well-spoken man of the world. This myth had been introduced to Russian culture in the late eighteenth century by Nikolay Karamzin, who had asserted, in a famous article, 'Why Russia Has So Few Literary Talents' (1802), that without proper access to polite society it was hard for a writer to educate his taste, however learned he might be.

In late eighteenth- and early nineteenth-century Russia, the reading of literature was an obligatory polite accomplishment for both men and women; indeed, writing itself was perceived as an agreeable social skill. Large numbers of women in the aristocracy and gentry kept an *al'bom*, a mixture of a scrap-book and a commonplace book, in which friends inscribed flattering verses (*madrigaly*), metrical tokens of love and friendship, and comic rhymes, next to sketched portraits and water-colour landscapes. Magazines and manuals gave models of appropriate pieces for albums (not having something ready to contribute when asked would have looked gauche). In such circumstances, the writing of poetry became an extension of polite conversation, a kind of refined game. Social convention demanded that verse offerings should in the main come from men and be addressed to women, and that the former should offer the latter flowery recognition of their beauty, intelligence, wit, and taste. For Karamzin, who had eulogized women's percipience and spiritual profundity in his *Epistle to*

Women (1796), the language of upper-class women should have been the model for Russian culture: in 'Why Russia Has So Few Literary Talents', he referred to 'those charming women [. . .] on whose conversation we might hope to eavesdrop in order to embellish a novel with genteel and felicitous expressions'.

Women, then, were perceived as ideal readers – at least of certain kinds of literary material – and as exponents of the brilliant conversation which prose writers sought to imitate in their novels. The particular place in which this perception was enacted was the *zala* or the *gostinaya*, the saloon or drawing-room in a private house or apartment. Throughout the late eighteenth, nineteenth, and early twentieth centuries, it was customary for prominent figures in society, many of them women, to keep open house on one day a week. Writers and musicians would be invited to perform their works in front of the visitors, who might include other artists and distinguished foreigners as well as members of the Russian social elite. One of the most famous such 'salons' (as they came to be known in the late nineteenth century) took place in the Moscow house of Princess Zinaida Volkonskaya during the early 1820s: Pushkin was among the writers who attended, and who penned respectful tributes in the hostess's album.

It is important, though, not to exaggerate the significance of the salon as a literary institution (as opposed to an instrument of polite culture more broadly, a place where men might acquire 'that particular tenderness of spirit and taste that many hold to be the especial gift of women', in the phrase used by a conduct book translated into Russian in 1765). In early nineteenth-century Russia, as opposed to sixteenth- and seventeenth-century France, mixed company was not the place for heavyweight literary discussion (such as might take place between men when on their own), but rather for light-hearted banter and flirtatious verbal fencing. Artists would perform pieces likely to be successful in such a setting (witty and brilliant, rather than profound). Though salon

15. Pushkin declaiming his verses to the 'Green Lamp' literary society. This kind of all-male gathering was the preferred forum for serious new work throughout the salon era.

hostesses themselves sometimes treated the company to their own compositions (as in the case of Volkonskaya), for the most part the female contribution consisted of marriageable young women showing off their accomplishments as singers or players on the pianoforte (as in Jane Austen's fictional drawing-rooms). Once Romanticism had brought to Russia the idea of art as a sacred activity that should be received in reverence and mute sympathy by readers, viewers, or listeners, participation in the salon became increasingly irksome to artists. When irritated by persistent requests to perform a party piece in Volkonskaya's salon, Pushkin is alleged to have responded with a recitation of 'The Poet and the Mob', his assault on the stupidity of readerly expectation. (The accuracy of this story is questionable, since Volkonskaya left Russia in 1828, and the poem also dates from that year, but the fact that the anecdote had currency is an indicator of prevailing attitudes.) And in *A Double Life* (1846), a novella by mid-nineteenth-century Russia's most talented female Romantic poet, Karolina Pavlova, poets give recitals in the heroine's mother's drawing-room to an artistically ignorant public who consider art a distraction from the main business of the day – contriving a lucrative match.

As Pavlova's story indicates, by the 1840s polite culture and literary culture were seen as more or less completely incompatible, a shift in taste to which the rise of the heavyweight literary journal (or 'fat journal', as it was affectionately known in Russian) made a significant contribution. The editorial boards of such journals were invariably made up of individuals with strong political views, whether radical or conservative; literary texts appeared alongside political commentary (or were themselves a form of disguised political commentary). Genres such as the 'madrigal', or the 'society tale', representing the difficulties of expressing feeling while observing propriety, did not suit the new era. Tastes ran more to ballads of working-class Russian life, stirring tales of women's liberation, and depictions of peasant suffering. Poetry of emotional attachment became a marginal genre. Both Aleksey Tolstoy and Karolina Pavlova composed fine poems dedicated to the theme of 'forbidden love', but from the 1850s such material was generally the prerogative of the drawing-room romance, a genre whose cultural authority, such as it was, came from its musical setting rather than its literary connections. By the early twentieth century, those whose verses made their way into romance tradition were minor figures, such as 'G. Galina' (pen-name of Glafira Mamoshina), or 'K. R.' (pen-name of Grand Duke K. K. Romanov). Though their work was very popular, the standing of such individuals with the literary establishment was low. In 1915, Marietta Shaginyan (later a Socialist Realist novelist, but then a minor Modernist poet) rebuked her friend, the composer Rachmaninov, for his dreadful taste in poems (his early song-cycles had set work by, for instance, Galina), and persuaded him to use material of more literary ambition in his next cycle of songs.

To be sure, the Russian Modernists did have salons of their own. But these were not remotely like the upper-class gatherings of the past, or like the grand St Petersburg and Moscow drawing-rooms of the late nineteenth and early twentieth centuries. In the household of Zinaida Gippius and Dmitry Merezhkovsky, talk turned to spiritualism, the occult, and mystical religion; at the Wednesday assemblies held in the top-floor apartment of Vyacheslav Ivanov, known as 'The Tower', guests sprawled on velvet cushions in rooms draped with exotic fabrics. Extravagance of this kind did not long survive the Russian Revolution, but even in the Soviet Union there were some prominent writers who presided over gatherings not unlike alternative salons. Anna Akhmatova, for instance, bestowed on favoured visitors her aphoristic comments about literature, art, and the literary personalities of her day; the Socialist Realist writer Vera Panova, who held high office in the Union of Writers, was beset by guests wanting not only good sense and racy talk, but also – if they could get them – letters of introduction to publishing houses.

In the Modernist circles and artistic cabarets that proliferated in Moscow and St Petersburg during the 1910s, though, unconventionality was the main cultural value. Their very names – 'The Wandering Dog', 'The Players' Tavern' – underlined the fashion for bohemian marginality. Like high society in the early nineteenth century, this was a culture where 'all the world was a stage', where people valued assured performance more than they did sincerity; but the roles enacted by artists were now considerably more extravagant than they had been in the 1820s and 1830s, when writers had been less cut off from the world of the court and the civil service, and when the standing of actual actors had been much lower. (The late nineteenth and early twentieth century had seen a number of players, notably the 'Russian Eleonara Duse' Vera Komissarzhevskaya, attain a considerable cultural authority in the literary world.) But above all, in a world where life was supposed to imitate art, it had become vital to express creativity through eccentric behaviour as well as through a contempt for artistic and linguistic formulae, for the 'clichés' that Russian Modernists despised as much as the French Modernists from whom many of their theoretical appreciations ultimately derived. In other words, it was idiosyncratic conduct that was now required, rather than the subordination to universally recognized ethical and aesthetic constraints that had been the central demand of participants in mixed literary gatherings during the early nineteenth century.

Pushkin, though, was writing in an era when the relationship between literature and polite culture was still taken for granted, even if it was beginning to break down. He was one of the last major Russian writers to participate in aristocratic salons of the kind organized by Zinaida Volkonskaya (just as she was one of the last female aristocrats who was at any level a serious artist). Several of Pushkin's writings – *Egyptian Nights*, *Evgeny Onegin*, the novel fragment 'The Guests Assembled at the Dacha' (1828–30) – use the aristocratic salon as a setting for central scenes. The urbane tone cultivated in polite society was one of the registers routinely employed by the poet (as is shown by 'And don't dispute with fools'). Some of his most famous poems have the brilliant conventionality required by the salon (an example is the famous love

16. Pushkin, doodled self-portrait in female dress. The poet made no attempt to flatter his unladylike profile: the effect of seeing it emerge from the bun and ringlets is amusingly incongruous.

poem 'I remember the wonderful moment:/You appeared before me/ Like a fleeting vision', which was to have a long drawing-room afterlife as a romance set to music by Glinka). Pushkin followed Karamzin, too, in his intensive interest in the psychology and language of women: this can be seen not only in the prominence of female protagonists in his work, but also in the fact that some of his 'costumed confessions' were made in female dress (as with the last line of 'Monument', where the advice to avoid demeaning squabbles fits with contemporary expectations that ladies remain calm under all circumstances).

At the same time, though, the inspiration that the salon offered Pushkin was often fused with unease, or even irritation, at the limits of polite language, and particularly at the demand that strong emotion be voiced in a safely conventional way. This unease can be sensed in another very famous love poem, 'I loved you' (1829):

> I loved you; love as yet, perhaps
> Has not burned out in my heart;
> But may it trouble you no longer,
> I do not wish to sadden you with anything.
> I loved you wordlessly, hopelessly,
> Tormented now by timidity, now by jealousy;
> I loved you so sincerely, so tenderly,
> As God grant you be loved by another.

This poem is quintessentially 'Pushkinian' in its dignified plainness and apparently self-explanatory directness; it is sometimes used (not wholly accurately) as an instance of the poet's distaste for metaphor. But in fact, there is a good deal more here than first meets the eye or the ear. Among many buried associations is the point that the opening lines of the poem evoke 'feminine language' – the new language of the emotions that Sentimentalism had seen as women's particular domain. Great rhythmic emphasis is placed on verbs such as 'to trouble' and 'to sadden', as well as on the metaphor of love as flame (this hackneyed image is delicately suggested through the verb 'to burn out', usually used of lamps or candles). The second half of the poem opposes to these conventional verbs and figures of speech a hyperbolic evocation of unutterable love, emotionally inarticulate, yet also the gift of a (masculine) Deity. The use of religious language in the final line is far from incidental, since this language stands both for sincerity and for 'Russianness' in the later Pushkin (as, for example, in one of his last poems, 'Desert fathers and immaculate women' (1836)). The effect is that 'masculine' sincerity displaces what can be seen, once the poem's narrative is complete, as charming, 'feminine' artifice. The 'feminine' vocabulary of affect becomes the starting point rather than the end of inspiration. Its particularity is opposed to the universality of the 'masculine' religious text. Evoking feminine language, Pushkin at the same time refuses to be limited by it: 'I loved you' moves from ventriloquism of the beloved's speech to assertion of another and very different set of linguistic values.

Pushkin was no misogynist. The writer would have been shocked to hear such a suggestion: in his day, the typical misogynist was a surly country squire or boorish merchant who thought that education would turn girls into bad wives, and believed it 'unchristian for any grown man to sit at the feet of a female'. Traces of this attitude can be found in the work of some early nineteenth-century writers, including talents as brilliant as Gogol, but not in Pushkin's own poetry or fiction, which is notable for its finely drawn and sympathetic portraits of women (the inspiration to women writers as well as men). But it is hard to argue with a historian who, after sifting through all the writer's essays, reviews, and jottings, concluded that Pushkin (like many of his contemporaries) unreservedly admired only one woman author, Madame de Staël. There is a striking contrast, too, between the roles played by male and female addressees in his letters, verse epistles, and dedications to published works (the latter are the subjects of gallantry sometimes tinged with eroticism, while the former cover a far wider range, from confidants to debating partners, from rivals to confederates in debauchery).

To argue along these lines does not mean placing Pushkin on a list of writers deserving critical annihilation, summoning him before what one senior American Slavist, writing in 1994, sarcastically termed 'the stern tribunal of assistant professors'. Gender-aware criticism does not have to amount to ideologized proscription. Nor – to rebut another hostile argument occasionally used against it – does it require the imposition of modern views on texts from different eras. 'Feminism' refers to a geographically and historically limited phenomenon (a European movement, or series of movements, beginning in the sixteenth century). But sexual difference and sexual acts are an abiding obsession in all human societies. There is no evidence whatever that Pushkin was interested in, or even aware of, the feminism of his day (it is most unlikely that he had read, say, Mary Wollstonecraft's *A Vindication of the Rights of Women*). He could not have anticipated the theories of Gayatri Spivak or Hélène Cixous, any more than he could those of Marx and Lenin. But he was without doubt passionately interested in issues of sex and gender, in what he, along with most educated people of his day, considered an obvious but fascinating and awkward truth, that men and women were immutably different.

This opinion, and its corollary, the belief that feminine language and experience had particular significance, masculine language and experience universal significance, were also held by many female contemporaries of Pushkin's. Evdokiya Rostopchina, for example, in her poem 'Pushkin's Notebook' (1839), described the book not in order to suggest a sort of equivalence between Pushkin's unpublished texts and the reluctance of women writers to enter print, but in order to underline the inferiority of feminine writing: 'I am a woman! My intellect and inspiration/Should be bound by humble modesty.' The poem ended with an apology that Rostopchina had dared to offer her 'timid song' in place of 'Pushkin's wondrous verse': the two alternative paraphrases of the word 'poetry', 'song' and 'verse', emphasized the distance between the masculine and the feminine text.

The assumption that 'masculine' expression or experience was universal, and 'feminine' expression or experience restricted in import, was a persistent force in nineteenth- and twentieth-century Russian culture. Women writers were associated first and foremost with certain well-defined cultural roles, above all the expression of emotion and the provision of guidance in personal ethics. To put it schematically, male writers were believed to offer enlightenment (*prosveshchenie*), women writers moral indoctrination (*vospitanie*). This belief could provide women writers with a strong sense of personal mission (as expressed, for instance, in Akhmatova's resolute opposition to state-sanctioned murder, or in the determination of memoirists such as Nadezhda Mandelstam or Evgeniya Ginzburg to act as witnesses to their times). A rather less considerable benefit was that it allowed women to become the voice of 'Communist morality' in the Socialist Realist novel. But although women writers could gain stature from conventional ideas about feminine identity, at the same time, if their writings were too concerned with the private sphere, which was perceived as women's particular area of power, they were certain to attract criticism – as happened in the case even of orthodox Socialist Realist writers, such as Vera Panova. Long before Soviet censorship made producing work for the 'desk drawer' routine for all writers, women writers made a habit of this; they were also much more likely to publish anonymously or to adopt pseudonyms than men, and to present their writings as 'found texts' (publishing what was actually an original piece of fiction as though this were the diary of a tragically deceased young woman lately discovered in the secret drawer of her desk).

But all this did not stop some women writers from asserting themselves as independent artists, particularly in the early twentieth century, an era when women's liberation was openly debated, and when critics sympathetic to feminism (for example, Elena Koltonovskaya and Zinaida Vengerova) took an explicit interest in women's creativity. Women writers were also helped by the Russian Symbolists' conviction that the human personality was androgynous in nature: now they could openly identify themselves with male predecessors, as well as female ones. 'Monument', interpreted as the testament of a beleaguered writer drawing comfort from the certainty of posthumous vindication, was a particular landmark for women poets who fiercely believed in their own unrecognized genius. (One such was Anna Akhmatova, as is shown by the passage from *Requiem* evoking her possible future monument that I quoted in Chapter 2.)

For all their aspirations to be treated as equals of their male contemporaries, however, it was still difficult for women writers to achieve elevation to the pantheon of literary greats, at any rate in critical commentaries with ambitions to evaluate the past rather than simply catalogue it. So, while women were well represented in bibliographies, and in the compilatory publications of positivist critics, such as V. V. Sipovsky's two-volume *History of the Russian Novel* (1909), they (unlike minor male writers of the eighteenth and early nineteenth century) were largely excluded from the writings of the most brilliant group of early twentieth-century theorists, the Russian Formalists. The reasons for this lay in some of the Formalists' governing assumptions about literary evolution, which they saw as driven by the efforts of a talented writer or writers. A gifted writer was sensitive to 'automatization', or the slide of literary techniques into cliché, at the very moment when it began happening; he (to use the appropriate pronoun) could raise what Tynyanov called 'paraliterature' (*literaturnyi byt*) to the level of real literature. Despite the Formalists' own preferred term for their work, 'descriptive poetics', what they produced was really an interpretive poetics. Thus they were able to combine a detestation of biographical criticism ('laundry list scholarship') with reverence for the achievements of selected individuals – Derzhavin, Pushkin, Dostoevsky, Tolstoy, Tyutchev, Evgeny Baratynsky, and Konstantin Batyushkov (their main alteration to the canon of their own days at university was the admission of writers close to Pushkin, such as these last two). Women's writing was not explicitly accounted for in any of the evolutionary models, but in practice it was usually assigned to the status of 'paraliterature'. For example, Lidiya Ginzburg's authoritative study of nineteenth-century Realism, *On Psychological Prose* (1971), contrasted the talented *writing* of the political thinker and memoirist Aleksandr Herzen with the talented *personality* of his wife Natalya (also the author of autobiographical writings, but ones, Ginzburg apparently considered, of documentary rather than literary value).

The assumption of a hard-and-fast distinction between 'literature' and 'everyday language', 'literature' and 'paraliterature', effaced from view, in Formalist and post-Formalist criticism, the importance of mixed-genre texts in the work of women writers, such as the diary in verse (to be found in Rostopchina's work as well as that of Akhmatova), and the significance in women writers' work of paraliterary citations, such as references to everyday speech (for instance, the mundane comments of an unfaithful lover in Akhmatova's early poetry). And, while Formalist critics' disdain for biography was helpful to the study of women's writing in some ways (Eikhenbaum's brilliant 1923 study of Akhmatova, for instance, eschewed clichés about 'feminine poetry' in favour of a close reading of literary devices in her work), it meant that women writers could not be studied as women. Therefore, questions about whether literary devices had a different resonance when located in a text that was linguistically marked as feminine (by the use of feminine adjectives and verbal forms, say) remained unasked. Equally, the importance of biographical realia for many women writers (and indeed for male writers such as Blok and Mayakovsky, for whom the tortured masculine self was a major theme) was ignored. Akhmatova's *Poem Without a Hero*, her great retrospective narrative poem about the 'start of the twentieth century' in 1913, is quite incomprehensible without some knowledge of the personalities in the poet's circle, and the poet's own experience, just as is Tsvetaeva's *Poem of the End*; both Akhmatova and Tsvetaeva maintained personal cults of Pushkin not only as artist, but also as man, producing vehemently subjective and partisan accounts of his marriage to Natalya Goncharova. It is interesting to note as well that Tsvetaeva, in her essay 'The Poet and the Critic', mounted

an open attack on Formalism, claiming that all her work was an attempt
to represent the world and had nothing to do with 'formal tasks' in the
abstract.

The 'Big Four' of Russian Poetry

Anna Akhmatova (1889–1966), Boris Pasternak (1890–1960),
Osip Mandelstam (1891–1938), and Marina Tsvetaeva (1892–
1941) were four of the greatest poets of the twentieth century.
All four suffered persecution under the Soviet regime. Mandelstam died in a prison camp in 1938; Akhmatova's first husband,
Nikolay Gumilyov, was executed in 1921, and her son and third
husband were imprisoned during the Great Purges, as were
Tsvetaeva's husband and daughter; Pasternak was subjected to
vilification after the publication of *Dr Zhivago*, and the award to
him of the Nobel Prize. At the same time, because all four
(unlike, say, Nabokov) died in Russia, they could be discussed in
public and republished during the post-Stalin era. In Western
writings about Russian literature, the four are often grouped
together as though they were members of a kind of informal
but exclusive circle, something along the lines of the
Bloomsbury group. Yet no group photograph or portrait of the
four exists (in fact, there was never an occasion when all were in
the same place at once). And while Akhmatova and Mandelstam were linked by lasting friendship, the same cannot be said
about any of the others (Tsvetaeva and Mandelstam had a
short-term affair, but lost contact after Tsvetaeva's emigration;
Tsvetaeva and Pasternak's relationship was intense, but carried
on by letter, and most of the emotion was on Tsvetaeva's side;
Akhmatova and Pasternak felt at most wary respect for one
another; Akhmatova and Tsvetaeva's relations were decidedly
strained). On the other hand, there were several other figures

who were close in one way or another to at least one of the group – for example, Vladimir Mayakovsky, a major influence on Tsvetaeva and the addressee of a tribute by Akhmatova. The association, then, is as much a matter of myth as fact, helped along by a line of Akhmatova's, 'There aren't many of us, three or four, maybe', and also, perhaps, by the musical parallels in this combination of two male and two female voices, all with their own distinct timbres – like a four-part ensemble in one of Mozart's operas, with Akhmatova playing mezzo to Tsvetaeva's soprano, and Mandelstam tenor to Pasternak's bass-baritone.

Women writers, then, did not necessarily fit any better into the analytical paradigms of Formalism than they did into politically engaged perceptions of writers as 'masters of minds'. Since Formalism was, from the early 1960s, once again to be the single most dominant trend in the serious study of Russian literature, among Western critics as well as Russian ones, the rise of gender-oriented criticism in Britain, America, France, and Scandinavia during the 1970s at first had little impact on critical practices or on university courses, even in the West. However, in the mid-1980s, a few Western Slavists, mostly in America, started to make a systematic attempt to recover work by women writers. Barbara Heldt's *Terrible Perfection* (1987) contrasted male writers' suffocating view of women's innate moral superiority with women writers' own struggle to represent a richer and more challenging understanding of female identity. The *Dictionary of Russian Women Writers* (1994), edited by Marina Ledkovsky, Charlotte Rosenthal, and Mary Zirin, brought hundreds of forgotten authors back to scholarly attention. By the late 1990s, the work of these and other writers had managed to create something approaching an alternative canon of Russian literature, one made up of women writers and shaped by a strongly individualist stress on self-assertion and self-examination (that is, on various forms of autobiography or fictionalized autobiography). Newly discovered or rediscovered writers included Karolina Pavlova, the early nineteenth-century poet Anna Bunina, the twentieth-century lesbian poet Sofiya Parnok, and the nineteenth-century prose writer Nadezhda Durova, author of the transvestite memoir *The Memoirs of a Cavalry Maid*. The priorities of gender criticism also inspired important re-readings of established writers, especially Tsvetaeva, who emerged as a pioneer of writing by Russian women about the female body.

At times, to be sure, a new kind of critical elision took place, this time of writers who could not easily be presented as proto-feminist rebels. A case in point was Rostopchina: one American feminist critic, for example, wrote of her 'inordinate preoccupation [with] parties and dancing' and her frivolous attitude to literature ('writing for her [. . .] had the appeal of an agreeable hobby'). Yet there are grounds for arguing that Rostopchina's pose of female dilettantism and modesty was in fact a way of facilitating entry to the potentially 'immodest' world of writing. In circumstances where the publication by women of literary work (as opposed to the production of poems, stories, and memoirs for circulation among close family and friends) was seen as tantamount to sexual exhibitionism if not prostitution, the adoption of a modest mask (a mask that was sometimes misleading in terms of a writer's actual character) was a form of social insurance, and one that could sometimes allow women to write with impunity on 'unfeminine' subjects.

At the same time, the historicist argument should perhaps not be pressed too far: a critical reading that limits itself to working within the intellectual universe of a given literary text *as consciously expressed*, rather than attempting to explore deeper shades of meaning and nuance, can turn into a tautologous paraphrase and runs the risk also of smoothing out aberrant or dissonant elements. If one sees Rostopchina's 'Pushkin's Notebook' as nothing more than a docile recognition of feminine inferiority (albeit one that was expedient, because it allowed Rostopchina to speak in the first place), one might miss the fact that, in describing women as 'bound' (*skovany*) by modesty, Rostopchina uses an adjective that was customarily applied to Prometheus, whose rebellion against patriarchal control had made him a model for pre-Romantic and Romantic young men, from Goethe to Shelley. It is perhaps unlikely that Rostopchina *intended* to compare herself to Prometheus; however, it is possible that her choice of vocabulary unconsciously took issue with the prevailing view of tortured genius as necessarily masculine. Obviously, it would be foolish to base an entire interpretation of the poem on this one word, but the example illustrates that even a studiedly conventional text may on occasion 'deautomatize' language. Wrenched from its customary context, a cliché is not necessarily a cliché.

It is this variety of feminist criticism, one sensitive to linguistic nuance in Formalist tradition but also to historical and biographical context, that began to be practised among some Russian and Western critics in the late twentieth century. By the late 1990s, too, there were beginning to be signs of a shift in the standing of women writers in their homeland. They still might not (with the exception of Akhmatova) have their monuments, or (with the exception of Tsvetaeva, or again Akhmatova), their museums, but writers were beginning to be republished in Russia, as well as outside: Sofiya Parnok, Adelaida Gertsyk, Alla Golovina, and Zinaida Gippius were only four of the writers who now had book-length editions to themselves. To be sure, suspicion of *feminizm* remained widespread, a hangover from the Soviet Union's cultural isolation (Russian writers and critics, unlike some of their counterparts in Poland, Yugoslavia, or the German Democratic Republic, had little direct access to Western cultural theory of any kind before the late 1980s), but also a result of ingrained suspicion of psychobiography; the feeling that *feminizm* was alien was not helped by the crudity of some early Russian attempts to propagandize it (blundering attacks on *Lolita* as pornography and the like). But as increasing familiarity with new kinds of cultural theory began to enliven and enrich the study of Russian literature inside Russia, which had endured something of a conceptual stasis for the last two decades of the twentieth century, and as the spread of post-Modernist ideas made the expression of a particular and partial, eccentric and individual, perspective a reputable choice for all writers, not just biographically female ones, a greater tolerance for women's 'marginal' explorations of the self became possible. Symptomatic was the appearance of a serious and careful discussion of Western scholarship on women's writing in the liveliest Russian literary-critical journal, *New Literary Review*, in 1997. All in all, the posthumous monument for which generations of Russian women writers had longed, an intellectual rather than a stone one, was beginning to seem, for at least some of them, a real possibility. Unlike some of the critical approaches discussed in this book, gender-aware criticism had never pretended to be the only proper or legitimate approach to literary texts, to offer final answers. It did not rank writers in terms of their 'progressivity' in feminist terms. But it could reasonably claim to have raised a new and interesting set of *questions*, and to have demonstrated (something that writers themselves had always known) that masculine and feminine identity was no more obvious or easy to understand than any other aspect of the human self as reflected in literature.

Chapter 7

'Every tribe and every tongue will name me'

Russian literature and 'primitive culture'

The 'Russians' are no more than a group of specialists in the Russian language.

(M. L. Gasparov, 2000)

'Monument' envisaged that Pushkin's name would be known not only in Europe, but in Asia. The poet predicted a readership from among Russia's subject tribes: the Poles ('proud descendants of the Slavs'), the Finns (the Grand Duchy of Finland had been added to Russia in 1800), the Tungus (now known as the Evenki, an indigenous people of Siberia), and the Kalmyks (from the area north of the Caucasus, on the shores of the Caspian Sea). Had Pushkin been gifted with the powers of geopolitical prophecy, he might have added the Uzbeks, the Kazakhs, and the Kyrgyz, since during the Soviet period compulsory Russian teaching in schools throughout the Soviet Union meant that the vast majority of citizens, whatever their ethnic affiliation, had heard the name of Pushkin.

The fact that the peoples of Central Asia are not included in Pushkin's list of 'tribes' is easy to explain: the first Russian conquests there took place only in the mid-nineteenth century, and the region was not fully subjugated until the 1880s. But the list was not exhaustive even in terms of the Russian Empire of Pushkin's day. 'The Finns' stand also for the Balts (Estonians, Latvians, Lithuanians), and the Georgians and Armenians are not mentioned. This selection of ethnic groups is not at all accidental. Reference to the Georgians and the Armenians, literate peoples with a long history of Christianity, would have unsettled Pushkin's representation of his poetry as a means of transmitting civilized values to savage peoples (the adjective 'savage' is in fact applied to the Tungus in 'Monument'). Entertaining a Byronic fascination with Oriental exoticism in his early twenties, Pushkin had, from the point at which he wrote *The Gypsies* (1824), taken an ironical view of this, seeking to play down picturesque differences of ethnicity. The conclusion of *The Gypsies* stresses the universality of moral problems:

> And everywhere are fatal passions,
> And there is no salvation from destiny.

An elder Gypsy proves an Enlightenment raisonneur who, quaintly, has even heard of Ovid (though not by name: he knows him only as a political exile banished from the Roman South to the Caucasian 'North'). Still more striking is the muting of local colour through detail chosen for its relative mundanity. The Gypsy retinue includes a shackled dancing-bear such as might have been seen in many Russian villages; it is Aleko, the outsider, who is a wide-eyed idealist, his Gypsy wife Zemfira who acts out of practical self-interest. Similarly, in his travelogue *Journey to Erzerum* (1829), Pushkin wearily recorded the tedious difficulties of passing through the Caucasus: the unreliable transport and rapacious drivers; the dirty hotels and unattractive women; the sustained hostility of the Turks and the Caucasian tribesmen. The heroism and uprightness of the invading Russian forces can only emerge to advantage by comparison; the emphasis on the prospect of salvation through military intervention is the major difference between this text and Alexander William Kingslake's *Eothen* (1841), the jaded tone being common to both. In the words of the linguist and scholar Peter France, *Journey to Erzerum* 'pulls the carpet from under the Romantic primitivism of much Caucasian writing [. . .] meant as a parody of Châteaubriand's *Itinéraire de Paris à Jerusalem*, it mocks the clichés of such travel literature'. At the same time, the text was in tune with the official ideologies of expanding Russian imperialism, according to which, in the geographer Mark Bassin's words, the 'stagnation' with which Asia was credited 'appeared to offer a suitably backward contrast to the creative and progressive dynamism of the West, a dynamism which Russia now claimed as its own'.

Yet so far as the imaginative world of Empire went, *Journey to Erzerum* was aberrant (as Pushkin himself seemed to sense: the text was published only in part before his death). Jean-Jacques Rousseau's belief in the 'noble savage' still seduced many in the 1830s and 1840s; and the search for the exotic that characterized Romantic literature everywhere was, in Russia turned inward and applied to those parts of the Empire that had been colonized recently enough to have maintained a strong and sometimes threatening local identity. Of these, the most attractive were the Crimea, and especially the Caucasus, which had the virtue of combining an 'Oriental' flavour with the spectacular scenery that had attracted Western searchers for the picturesque to the Alps. Pushkin himself, in *Prisoner of the Caucasus* (1822) and *Fountain of Bakhchisarai* (1823), had relocated Byronic dramas of erotic fascination and cultural entanglement from the Ottoman Empire to the Crimea and the Caucasus. Of the two texts, the more seductive for many modern readers is *The Fountain of Bakhchisarai*. The central conflict (a jealous intrigue in the harem) is not only more fully developed in psychological terms, but lays bare powerful myths about women as the symbols of national identity (a fiery and dusky Georgian is pitted against a virtuous blonde Pole, as symbol of Western Europe). Moreover, the verse is not only beautifully lush but free of the Byronic cliché (mountains as 'kings of the wilds', and so on) that is calqued in *Prisoner of the Caucasus*. But it was the latter poem that was the more significant for Pushkin's contemporaries: indeed, the poem can be said to have initiated the literary 'discovery of the Caucasus'. Readers were enraptured by the lengthy descriptions of customs, dress, and manners (borrowed from printed sources, but interpreted at the time as first-hand ethnography), and the mysterious, impassive hero whose strange malaise is healed by his stretch in picturesque capitivity. The poem, in the words of Susan Layton, author of a pioneering book on Russian colonial texts, encouraged a 'restorative tourism focused on the self', setting out a 'romantic imaginative geography' of Russia's South that was to be drawn upon by countless other writers during the next three decades. Undoubtedly, Pushkin's own exotic origins on his mother's side (his great-grandfather Hannibal, 'the Moor of Peter the Great', was an African) helped establish his credibility as the portrayer of this 'imaginative geography': the publishers of the first edition of *A Prisoner of the Caucasus* used a swarthy, 'Moorish' picture of Pushkin as a child to illustrate the book. (Ill. 17.)

As this case shows, publishers, critics, and readers were apt to confuse authors and heroes, a confusion against which the author's preface to Lermontov's *Hero of Our Time* (1841) issued an irritable and timely warning. Partly this was because the myth of 'restorative tourism' itself tended to play on disguise motifs. John Buchan's Sandy Arbuthnot (Scottish gentleman, 'Greenmantle', and dervish prophet) and Rudyard Kipling's Mowgli, brought up by animals, had a quaint precursor in the eponymous hero of Aleksandr Bestuzhev-Marlinsky's *Ammalat-Bek* (1832), the perfect tribesman who was in fact Russian by descent. The ultimate figure of Russian Orientalist fantasy was the Circassian, a mountain man and daredevil rider of astonishing bravery, leading a life of frugal pastoralism enlivened with bandit raids. This alternative world was not at all like the dangerously effeminate sphere of the bathhouse and the harem that was evoked in *The Fountain of Bakhchisarai*, enclosed and self-indulgent, or like the Russian Orientalism of the eighteenth century, lambasted by Derzhavin in his masterpiece of irony *Felitsa*, which showed the grandees of Catherine's court lolling on velvet sofas in their silk robes, puffing at hookahs. The appeal of 'manly' and incorruptible Circassians to nineteenth-century Russian travel writers

17. Igor Geitman, engraving after anonymous drawing of Pushkin as a small boy. Heavy cross-hatching gives Pushkin a dark-skinned, 'African' appearance.

closely resembled the cult of the Bedouin among British visitors to Arabia in the first half of the twentieth century (for example, T. H. Lawrence and Wilfred Thesiger). The characteristic Romantic fascination with what could not be obtained applied itself here to the relationship between cultures as well as that between men and women: the ultimate object of desire perpetually defied possession. At the same time, tribes who resisted the project of colonization in which writers were themselves embroiled lent especial lustre to the process of subjugation: the valour of the invaders enhanced in proportion to the dangers associated with invasion. In the words of Susan Layton, the Caucasus was not only a 'redemptive space', but also a 'killing field', the ultimate testing ground for the Russian officer's sword of honour.

At the same time, the more thoughtful Russian writers sensed subtleties and contradictions in Russia's relationship with 'subject peoples' that made them eschew costume-dramatic representations of the confrontation between 'civilization' and 'savage'. A case in point was the representation of the Cossacks, the traditional defenders of Russia's borderlands (in Gogol's fervently nationalist novel *Taras Bulba* they were shown holding the frontiers of Russia and Orthodoxy against the perfidious Poles). Contrary to nationalist myth, Cossack settlers in the Caucasus, rather than defending the front line between Russians and other ethnic groups, demonstrated how permeable it was. As a recent historian, Thomas Barrett, has wondered, 'How "Cossack", for example, was Iakov Alpatov of the Cossack village of Naur who twice fled for the mountains, converted to Islam, and formed a thieving band of Chechens and Cossacks in the 1850s that robbed farmsteads, stole cattle, and took captives, not only from Cossacks but also from Kalmyks and Nogais well into the steppe?'. These tensions of identity figure also in Tolstoy's novella *The Cossacks*, in which the protagonist, Alpatov, finds himself confronted with a culture that is just as 'Oriental' and insusceptible to the gaze of the outsider as a community in Turkey or Egypt might have been. And if here the boundary between 'Orient' and 'West' had simply moved slightly further eastwards (separating Alpatov,

18. A Circassian warrior: here the manly hero is portrayed by a
nineteenth-century British artist.

the city-dweller, from tribal culture as represented by local settlers, rather than local settlers from tribal culture), other texts called the very existence of such a boundary into question. The most original and touching character in Lermontov's *Hero of Our Time* is not the splenetic Pechorin, a close descendant of Benjamin Constant's *Adolphe*, but the inarticulate and intellectually commonplace Maksim Maksimych, a low-ranking army officer whose knowledge of local conditions has given him not only a brusque intolerance of 'lazy natives', but also an exquisitely tactful sensitivity to local beliefs. On the death of Pechorin's short-term Circassian mistress Bela, it is Maksim Maksimych who not only makes the practical arrangements for the burial, but who offers a moving epitaph to Bela herself:

> We buried her behind the fortress, by a stream and near the place where she was sitting that last time. Now the bushes have grown up round her grave, white acacia and elder. I wanted to put a cross up, but, well, you know, I felt a bit uncomfortable about it; after all, she wasn't a Christian . . .

There is a grating contrast between this passage and Pechorin's formulaically cynical verdict on Bela when he has tired of her: 'The love of a female savage is scarcely more appealing than that of a young lady of high society: the ignorance and simplicity of the one grow as boring as the coquetry of the other.' Even Pechorin's response to Bela's death is stereotypical: in the words of Maksim Maksimych, 'He raised his head and laughed . . . That laugh raised goosepimples all over me.' For all Pechorin's tribal play-acting, he remains as distant from the spirit of the mountains and from that of their inhabitants as does the dilettante 'travel writer' narrator who discovers Pechorin's journals and decides to make a literary sensation by publishing these, and who provides the second layer of commentary in Lermontov's multi-perspective novel.

Lermontov's novel, then, juxtaposed the Romantic dandy's pose of assimilation with the mundane man of action's respect for difference,

19. A Cossack soldier. Note the 'orientalized' appearance of this man and his wife, portrayed by a minor nineteenth-century Russian artist.

and the metropolitan gentleman's mourning of the supposedly impassable barrier between ethnic groups with the lower-class settler's conviction that such a barrier was an illusion. At the same time, Pechorin's own confrontation with the Caucasus and the world of the Orient was not straightforward: it ended with his death in Persia, and before that he was repeatedly threatened with physical and mental disintegration. As Susan Layton has pointed out, Russian writers found it more difficult to believe in the 'alterity of Orient' than did their counterparts in Western Europe (with the exception of Spain, one might add), because of their country's absorption of waves of invaders (the Pechenegs, the Tartars) and the assimilation of 'Orientals' into their own culture.

The labile, fluid character of Russian national feeling was never more clearly indicated than in the publication of the merchant Afanasy Nikitin's remarkable fifteenth-century account of his visit to India, *Voyage Beyond Three Seas*, in Karamzin's epoch-making *History of the Russian State* (1818). At the heart of a history that celebrated the creation of a puissant Russia stood a text ending with an almost exact transcription of the prayer spoken by converts to Islam. The publication of Nikitin's narrative in Karamzin's showed the uncertainty at the centre of Russian national identity and illustrated how the result of contact with 'the other' could be a sense of Russia's closeness to the East, rather than of the gulf between Russia as part of Europe and the further territories.

This sense of closeness had resonance not only in the foundation, during the 1820s, of an outstanding tradition of scholarly investigation directed at the languages and cultures of the Eastern Empire, but also in philosophy and in artistic representations, culminating in the 'Eurasianism' of the early twentieth century. Blok's important cycle of lyric poems 'At Kulikovo Field' (1908) was a highly original interpretation of a famous victory over the Tartars in 1380, a battle as crucial to triumphalist national history as Borodino (or, in English tradition, Agincourt). The imagery of Blok's cycle recalled not only the *Zadonshchina*, a late fourteenth-century text celebrating the victory at Kulikovo, but also *The Lay of Igor's Campaign*, a still more famous twelfth-century text eulogizing a glorious Russian defeat. This intertextual double-exposure was only one of many layers of ambiguity in a text whose perspective slipped between the fourteenth century and the time of its composition, and which – as was revealed by Blok's contemporaneous essay 'The People and the Intelligentsia' – was also intended as a lament for the 'infrangible boundary' between the 'Tatar' intelligentsia and the 'true Russian' lower classes.

In a sense, then, one could see Russian literature as at once colonial and post-colonial, speaking simultaneously from the viewpoint of conqueror and conquered. Nikolay Trubetskoy, the most original thinker in the Eurasian group, took a militantly relativist attitude to European culture – 'European culture is obligatory only for the group of nations that created it' – which was very much in the spirit of *négritude*, the self-assertion movement among Francophone African and West Indian intellectuals in the 1940s, and of African-American philosophy as well. For Trubetskoy, the diversity of Russian culture was a source of pride, as was the racial mixture in the Russian Empire. So far as landscape was concerned, though, the Eurasian sensibility was attracted to the familiar rather than the exotic. It was the steppe, rather than the impassable mountain ranges of the Caucasus, that had become the preferred imaginative space. Rivers, the only borders in the steppe, were seen not only as 'infrangible boundaries' between battle-lines, but also as frontiers that might be crossed by stealth, or used as trading routes. Exactly so was the Russian language, the primary symbol of national difference for a Westernized Russian such as Turgenev, now seen as permeable to the East, distinguished from other Slavonic languages by its capacity for absorbing Turkic loan-words and phonetics.

Ten years after writing 'On Kulikovo Field', Blok himself moved from seeing tragedy in the binary inheritance of Russian culture, 'Tatar' and

'Russian', to seeing this as a source of strength. His 1918 poem 'Scythians' (quoted here in Robin Kemball's translation) celebrated a tribe that had been seen since classical Greek times as the epitome of vigorous barbarism. The Scythians stood for the resurgent life of Russia, traditionally the bulwark against incursions from the East, but now threatening to overwhelm enfeebled Western civilization with its hybrid vitality:

> So, Russia – Sphinx – triumphant, sorrowed too –
> With black blood flows, in fearful wildness,
> Her eyes glare deep, glare deep, glare deep at you,
> With hatred and – with loving-kindness!
> Yes, so to love, as lies within our blood,
> Not one of you has loved in ages!
> You have forgotten that there is such love
> That burns and burning, lays in ashes!

The 'Scythian' side of Russia was implicitly associated, in Blok's representation, with the creation myth of the Russian Revolution, understood by the poet in his first and enthusiastic response to it as a coming to power of the formerly oppressed, 'barbarous' underclasses. The association was not peculiar to Blok. The history of representation of the East was intimately intertwined with that of representation of 'the people' (narod, a noun signifying both 'people' and 'nation'). In a culture where, as late as 1897, only 21 per cent of the population was literate, the divide between 'civilization' and 'barbarism' had sometimes been understood to map on to the division between 'Westernized' and 'native Russian'. With the rise of the Slavophile movement in the 1830s, the idea that cultivated Russians were foreigners in their own country became a cliché in literature and in journalism. There was a realization that the discovery of uncorrupted exoticism did not always require a visit to the Caucasus: it could also be found in the Russian countryside. In the 1820s, some Russian Romantic writers, like their counterparts in other European countries, began to see folk tales and folk songs as a source of inspiration for literary endeavour. At first, it was the motifs and plots, rather than the language and structure, of folkloric texts that provided the inspiration. Some of Pushkin's tales on folklore subjects (*skazki*), such as 'The Tale of the Priest and his Worker Balda' (1830), paraphrased subjects from oral tradition (the poet had himself noted material from informants when staying on his estate at Mikhailovskoe in the late 1820s) and were composed in a genteel approximation of popular speech. But others, such as *The Golden Cockerel* (1834), were taken from Western European sources, were written in verse rather than prose, and used the vocabulary and inflections of educated conversation. Like his fairy-tale narrative poem *Ruslan and Ludmilla* (1820), and like verse tales by his contemporaries and successors (for example, Pyotr Ershov's *Little Hunchback Horse*, 1834), Pushkin's *skazki* had the charming artificiality of Charles Perrault or Jeanne L'Héritier's reworkings of French folklore, such as *The Sleeping Beauty* and *Beauty and the Beast*.

But the actual daily life of the Russian peasantry – beset by disease, poverty, poor to non-existent education, and (before 1861) enserfment – did not incline writers to witty brilliance. On the contrary, from the late eighteenth century, Russian literature had a sentimental preoccupation with the sufferings of the Russian peasantry at the hands of cruel or callous landowners. The customary symbol of the dashing Russian officer as the romantic pioneer of civilization in the Caucasus had its antipode in the figure of the exploited lower-class woman, as evoked in, say, Karamzin's story *Poor Liza* (1792), showing a peasant girl betrayed by a selfish young man from the upper classes. To be sure, Pushkin's story 'The Station-Master' in his *Tales of Belkin* (1829) suggested that the relationship between an upper-class man and his mistress from 'the people' might be based on affect and mutual contentment rather than one-sided exploitation. But this was, from the point of view of the Russian radicals who began to dominate Russian literary production in the 1840s, not a tenable suggestion. Indeed, in the 1840s and 1850s serfdom was seen even by some conservatives as an institution that was intrinsically wrong. And in 1851, the radical poet Nikolai Nekrasov, the most talented among politically committed authors of verse, made a degraded and beaten peasant woman the symbol of his verse and emblem of his social sympathy:

> But early lay heavy upon me the shackles
> Of another, untender and unloved Muse,
> Of the sad travelling-companion of sad beggars,
> Beggars born for struggle, suffering, and labour –
> Of a weeping, lamenting and hurting Muse,
> Perpetually hungry, pleading in degradation,
> Whose only idol was gold.

The Emancipation of the Serfs in 1861 did not mitigate the emphasis on rural misery but rather enhanced it. To be sure, some writers, such as Tolstoy, took a Utopian view of the new relationship between landowners and peasants. The scenes on Lyovin's estate in *Anna Karenina* (1876–8) show the patriarchal peasant household as a model for a successful family in which husband and wife have complementary and fulfilled lives. Two decades before, in his 'Landowner's Morning' (1851), Tolstoy had shown an enthusiastic young Russian gentleman trying to introduce rational work methods to his serfs: now Lyovin learned from his freed peasants not only how to mow, but also how to look at life. Having been unable to allay his suicidal frustration by studying philosophy and theology in books, Lyovin was finally set on the path to equilibrium by hearing of the attitude to life of an old peasant who 'lived for his soul and remembered God'.

But eulogization of rural life was possible only in conditions where peasants' land-holdings afforded them a tolerable existence. The chaotic process of land reform not only bankrupted many landowners who had lived on estate incomes before 1861, but also subjected peasants to economic uncertainty, leaving some worse off than they had been before the reforms. A single bad season could spell destitution and famine. All of this was observed at close quarters by the educated employees of the new post-Emancipation institutions of rural administration, the *zemstva*, such as doctors and teachers, many of whom were sympathetic to Populism (*Narodnichestvo*), a movement aimed at bringing education and political enlightenment to 'the people' but also (and paradoxically) at preserving the traditional practices and values of peasant life. A flowering of ethnography (the systematic collection of folklore and recording of material culture and daily life) was accompanied by a burgeoning of fiction rich in ethnographical detail, but also in social pessimism. The critical-realist stories of writers such as Gleb Uspensky, Nikolay Uspensky, Valentina Dmitrieva, and later Vsevolod Garshin, Vladimir Korolenko, and Ekaterina Letkova, painted an unremittingly bleak portrait of the Russian village. The degradation represented was so extreme that it raised questions about how this could possibly be mitigated by social reforms. A later and particularly grim example of this tradition was Chekhov's story 'The Peasants', which went down extremely badly with populists of a more idealistic colouration, such as Tolstoy. In Chekhov's imaginary village, with its rubbish-strewn stream, squalid huts, and brutal human relationships, the only event distracting from the daily grind was an annual religious procession, received with a pious and hysterical fervour that had absolutely no relevance to the tenor of life for the remainder of the year. Significantly, the only 'human' characters in the story were a waiter and his family who had returned from years of life in the city.

The sense of rural devastation, of what was often termed the 'bestialization of the people', prompted a search for the picturesque in the far North of Russia, which had remained relatively untouched by serfdom and which was saved by its remoteness from the seasonal migration to cities that had (in the eyes of many Populists) tainted the regions nearer to Moscow and St Petersburg with urban ways. It was here above all that folklore collectors searched for the rituals, celebrations, spells, songs, and tales that they believed preserved traditions stretching back to pre-Christian times. But the region from which material emanated was in the end less important than its character. Writers of the late nineteenth and twentieth century, who sometimes collected ethnographical material themselves as well as turning to published anthologies of such material, were attracted above all by texts that underlined the difference between town and countryside. In the Symbolist poet Valery Bryusov's vivid story-monologue 'Masha', for example, the narrator was a peasant girl for whom traditional folkloric figures such as the house spirit were absolutely real physical presences:

> Oh, Ma'am, you can't imagine how good it is living in Yaroslavl, the only thing that worries you here is the conmen, but in the village there's so much to be afraid of: courtyard spirits, and house spirits, and demons, and arch-demons. Outside in the courtyard there's a spirit, and inside the house there's one too; the spirit in the courtyard has a face on him like the master's, and the one in the house is all hairy. If anyone goes out to feed the horses after nine, then the courtyard spirit, he spies it straight away. You can't just go out like that, you have to cough first . . .

As this example indicates, the language of narration was now as important as the material cited. The vitality of much early twentieth-century Russian prose was derived directly from popular speech (*prostorech'e*). The favoured genre was a first-person narrative that eschewed the norms of educated speech (this type of narrative was to be retrospectively named *skaz* by Russian Formalist critics: see for instance Boris Eikhenbaum's 1918 essay 'The Illusion of *skaz*'). Before the Revolution, the most outstanding exponent of *skaz* was Aleksey Remizov, whose more successful imitators included Evgeny Zamyatin and Olga Forsh. After the Revolution, though, the Remizovian school, whose procedures might be described as 'dialect ornamentalism', went into something of a decline, the causes of which lay not only in Remizov's emigration (he left for Berlin in 1921 and later settled in Paris), but also in the determinedly pro-urban standpoint of the early Soviet regime. However, *skaz* persisted in transmuted form. The working-class narrators of Mikhail Zoshchenko's stories, such as 'The Bathhouse', spoke in a patchwork of mangled clichés taken from political discourse of the day ('This isn't the Tsarist regime, you know!') and popular language of quite a different kind (*grekh odin*, literally 'nothing but sin', but approximately equivalent to 'no peace for the wicked'). And their structure drew on traditional folk narrative patterns, such as triple repetition (the narrator of 'The Bathhouse' tries three times to get hold of a wash-tub for himself) and the use of a rhetorical formula to begin and end the narrative and mark it off from surrounding speech ('The Bathhouse' starts with the wonderfully surreal sentence, 'They say, lads, that in America the bathhouses are ever so excellent'). At the same time, Zoshchenko's characters were more than sociological studies: they were also masks for the writer himself. As the literary critic Alexander Zholkovsky has argued, the constant social and sexual failures of the writer's fictional protagonists played on obsessive motifs in Zoshchenko's psychoanalytically inspired autobiography, *Before Sunrise*; rather than laughing at the inarticulacy and inadequacy of those he had invented, Zoshchenko was using their helplessness to render decent the exploration of his own self. One could add that his stories were quintessentially Modernist not only because they 'made the world strange' (to adopt the term used by the Formalist literary theorist Viktor Shklovsky), but also because they expressed a profound philosophical pessimism about the communicative function of language. The fact that Zoshchenko's main characters are so often not understood, so frequently *baffled* (in all senses) by the responses of others, reflects not only the petty tyrannies of early Soviet life, but the urban isolation that gripped those living in the world of Daniil Kharms, or indeed Samuel Beckett.

Just so in poetry, the sociological, aesthetic, and philosophical functions of *skaz* intertwined: folklore was no longer kept at one remove but used in order to assault old concepts of appropriate behaviour and expression. Tsvetaeva's verse tale *The Tsar-Maiden*, for instance, was a transexual narrative representing the love of an aggressive, manly princess for a mild-mannered young princely aesthete; *The Swain* showed the union of a peasant girl and vampire-lover as a sublime erotic experience. For Tsvetaeva, as for several other Symbolist and post-Symbolist women poets, appropriation of folklore was a means of breaking away from the constraints of 'women's poetry' in a traditional sense – poetry of unhappy love, elegant narcissism, and self-effacing creativity. Her poem 'The Muse' represented a woman at the borders even of rural society, a vagrant, perhaps even a drab and an outlaw:

No birth, no marriage certificates,
No forefathers, no 'bright falcon' [i.e. young man].
She goes tearing along,
Such a distance away!

Under the dusky eyelids
[Glows] gold-winged fire.
With a wind-beaten hand
She snatched – and forgot.

Her hem trails in the dirt,
Her shoes gape apart.
Not wicked, not kind,
But far-off: her own woman.

Without 'certificates' (of birth, of marriage), without a man to ensure her respectability, and with her hem trailing in the dirt (a proverbial image of sluttishness in the sexual sense too), Tsvetaeva's Muse could not have been more different from the decorous muses, with impeccable literary credentials, that figured in Akhmatova's poetry. What is more, here, as in Tsvetaeva's work as a whole, the polarization between 'acceptable' rural folklore and 'vulgar' urban folklore that ran through much work by other nineteenth- and early twentieth-century writers broke down. (Indeed, Tsvetaeva's imitations of the 'vulgar' genre of street ballad in her poetry of the early 1920s were considerably more refined than her poems drawing on rural folklore.) However, the poem is marked by the stylistic features that characterized Modernist pieces in the folkloric style: fixed epithets ('gold-winged fire'); negative constructions ('not wicked, not kind'); and the use of parallelism (see particularly the 'hem' and 'shoes' of lines 9–10). At the same time, the poem was a self-portrait, a statement of the poet's right to defy convention, to exist beyond the official scripts of 'birth and marriage certificates'.

The fact that Modernists' work in the folk style was much closer to authentic rural popular culture than the writings of the Russian Romantics was one reason why the early twentieth century also saw poetry by actual members of the Russian lower classes enter the literary mainstream for the first time. Where nineteenth-century 'peasant poets', such as Aleksey Koltsov, had been incidental curiosities, their twentieth-century successors, above all Nikolay Klyuev, were formidable aesthetic and intellectual presences. Klyuev fused the dialect and natural phenomena of the far North, his birthplace, with esoteric Eastern philosophy, the theology of sects such as the Flagellants and the Self-Castrators, and citations of epic from Finland to North America. His was an extraordinary and individual artistic vision, where death was 'a squall/rumbling on foam-filled wagons/to life's outer shore', where the classical muse was replaced by a skylark, or a whale breasting the Arctic swell, and where Lenin, a 'cedar frost in Spring', was evoked as emotionally as 'the crystal voice of whooper swans'. For his part, Klyuev's contemporary and sometime comrade-in-arms Esenin, though a less considerable poet, was, forty years after his death, to become the most popular poet in Russia, with a poem that lamented the loss of youth vanishing 'like white smoke from the apple trees' sung to the guitar in millions of hostels and private flats.

By and large, though, it was intellectual writers looking for alternative material, including a significant group of upper-middle-class women (Zinaida Gippius, Adelaida Gertsyk, Marina Tsvetaeva) who immersed themselves in folk lexis and in popular tradition. The proletarian poets of pre-revolutionary worker journals and post-revolutionary Proletcult groups inclined to a stylistically conventional late Romanticism of foundry sparks and burning furnaces. And Socialist Realism made incumbent on writers the use of a style that would be 'accessible to the mass reader' rather than based on the putative language of that reader in his or her pre-educated state: this curtailed experiments in *skaz* in prose and poetry alike. By the time that literary adventurousness resurfaced again, in the 1960s, the majority of the Russian population was living in towns, and rural Russia (transformed by mass literacy, radio, and later television) was no longer the storehouse of 'folk culture' it once had been. But *skaz* of a Zoshchenkian kind (based on urban popular speech) began to enjoy some popularity again, particularly among writers not publishing in Soviet official sources (where prohibitions on use of 'obscene language', that is, the swear-words found in just about every sentence of real popular speech, meant that street language could appear only in bowdlerized form). It was employed not only in neo-Realist studies of the Soviet and post-Soviet underworld, but also in texts of greater literary and philosophical ambition, such as Yuz Aleshkovsky's revenge narrative, *The Hand* (1980), in which the narrator's disgust at the official who purged his family during collectivization juxtaposes the miraculous beauty of the man's possessions to their owner, apostrophized as 'you heap of shit'.

Much of the discussion in this book has emphasized the centredness of Russian literary tradition, as expressed in the demands made by generations of critics that writing should serve a serious purpose, and in the dominance of an enduring canon of great writers celebrated by memorials, informal commemorations, and by successive educational systems. In Chapter 6, I argued that this centredness placed women writers at the borders of their culture, made them provincials in terms of the literary heritage, as it were. This chapter has shown that centredness had its limits. To be sure, Russian writers of the nineteenth and twentieth centuries inhabited an imperial mindset, one in which non-Russians were often seen as colourful ethnographical exhibits, as examples of quaint or amusing otherness. Yet at the same time, the geographical peripheries of empire, in particular 'the East', could serve to unsettle reflective Russians' conviction of their own identity, leading them to question the nature of distinctions between 'East' and 'West'. And in the second half of the nineteenth century, a search for the exotic *inside* Russian culture became common, with folklore now seen as a repository of attractively barbaric themes and language, rather than a store of material that had to be 'genteelized' before it could be admitted to polite culture. This transformation of the standing of folklore in turn allowed writers from beyond the educated male elite (peasants, women, ethnic minorities) to profit from their own marginality, to exploit a situation where 'provincialism' (in the transferred sense used above) became a mark of distinction, rather than a sign of inferiority.

Chapter 8

'O Muse, be obedient to the command of God'

The spiritual and material worlds

> Monuments don't turn out well in Russia (the ones to Nikolay Gogol and
> so on). That's because the only tolerable kind of monument we seem to
> be able to build is a chapel, with an icon lamp perpetually burning for
> 'the servant of God Nikolay'.
>
> (Vasily Rozanov, 1913)

In Pushkin's writing generally, God is not usually as prominent as he is in
'Monument'. Notable, for example, is the omission of any aspect of
Christian belief or practice from *Evgeny Onegin*, including even the
Lenten fasting and Easter feasting that would have been annual events
in the household of a real-life Larin family. (In the 1850s, a British visitor
to Russia described Holy Week as a time when 'the only sound that from
time to time broke the mournful stillness which reigned throughout the
house was the monotonous voice of the priest'.) A carefree Voltairean
in his early days, Pushkin was later embarrassed by his youthful
godlessness (as is indicated by his attempts to remove his irreverent
poem about the Virgin Mary, *The Gabrieliad*, from circulation). Yet he
also belonged to a generation where the eighteenth-century mistrust
of religious 'enthusiasm' was strong. Unlike his sister Olga, a fervent
believer and the author of religious poetry in French, he did not incline
to explicit statements of faith. To be sure, the theme of imminent death
figured largely in his later poems, some of which, such as 'Whether I
wander along the noisy streets' (1829), see choosing a resting-place as

the only way in which the will may be exercised. And several poems of 1836 juxtapose worldly power and religious feeling, which latter draws in the lyric hero despite his strong sense of personal sin (as the critic Sergey Davydov has argued, there is strong reason to suppose that these poems, including 'Monument', may have formed part of a poetic cycle round the theme of Holy Week).

Like most aspects of Pushkin's creation, the question of the extent to which the writer was an active believer is controversial. It became particularly so once Soviet censorship disintegrated: at this point the patriots who had fulminated against Andrey Sinyavsky's *Strolls with Pushkin* as a profanation of the writer's memory began an all-out promotion of Pushkin's Orthodox connections, using books, articles, pamphlets, and a specialized journal, *The Pushkin Era in the Light of Christian Culture*. It was above all Pushkin's late poetry of repentance that was used as evidence here. But the desire for faith that these texts unquestionably did express is not the same thing as religious faith in a direct sense. There seems little to justify even the more moderate claim for Pushkin as an instance of how 'theology in Russia [. . .] expressed itself through poetry'. Rather, he was a crucial figure in the creation of a secular Russian literature. His great poetic predecessors, Lomonosov and Derzhavin, were not only inspired directly by liturgical texts (as in Derzhavin's remarkable paraphrases of the Psalms), but built their grandest poetic edifices on a foundation of the liturgical language, Church Slavonic (so, for example, in Derzhavin's 'The Waterfall', a profoundly Christian meditation upon the transience of worldly power). Such magnificent sententiousness and theological self-declaration is not to be found in Pushkin's writings; indeed, the extent to which he was an active believer is neither evident nor, in the end, relevant, except perhaps to those the leftist writer and critic Osip Brik termed 'maniacs such as those passionately seeking the answer to the question "Did Pushkin smoke?"'. If Belinsky and his radical colleagues could consider Pushkin an 'encyclopedia' of Russian life, this was partly because spiritual matters were as marginal here as they were in the French

Encyclopédie. Bypassing Pushkin, the Russian tradition of metaphysical poetry was revived, after Derzhavin, by Pushkin's contemporaries Evgeny Baratynsky and Fyodor Tyutchev; it then resurfaced again – after decades of dormancy – in the 1890s, most notably in the poetry of the religious philosopher Vladimir Solovyov and his successor Vyacheslav Ivanov.

Pushkin's prose was still less accommodating to mystical matters than his poetry. His great contemporary, Nikolay Gogol, was far more openly pious, as was reflected, for example, in his moralistic correspondence with his mother and sisters. Yet even Gogol's beliefs remained curiously marginal to his works. To be sure, some of his stories have an affinity with Christian parable. Both *Old-World Landowners* (1835) and *The Overcoat* (1841) are intimately connected with an ascetic Christian critique of self-gratification and the accumulation of material possessions: in both, the 'mistake' made by the characters is not to 'lay up treasure in heaven', not to prepare for the inevitable day of divine judgement. But both texts, like Gogol's great novel *Dead Souls* and his play *The Government Inspector*, were the product of a talent that found sinfulness easier to imagine than virtue. The main character of *The Overcoat*, the pathetic Akaky Akakievich, with his scatological name (*kakat'* is a childish word for defecation, 'to cack') and his haemorrhoidal complexion, was a walking vision of fleshly disgust, someone who, like the characters in *Dead Souls*, was a corpse in Christian terms long before his death.

The search for an Orthodox revival in literature emerged in theory before it did in practice, then. It was expressed not only in Gogol's treatise *Selected Passages from Correspondence with Friends*, but also in the work of writers associated with the 'Slavophile' movement of national conservatives that began to emerge in the late 1830s – Ivan Kireevsky, Aleksey Khomyakov, and Konstantin Aksakov. Where radical writers were rabidly secular in their tastes, the Slavophiles looked back nostalgically to Russia before the time of Peter the Great, when, so they believed, religion had infused every aspect of secular life. The fact that imaginative literature was itself a Western concept (as I mentioned in Chapter 2, textual production in medieval Russia was dominated by ecclesiastical needs) did not worry the Slavophiles, since they believed it was possible to combine the best features of Western and native Russian 'enlightenment' (*prosveshchenie*). The culmination of their ideas, in a literary sense, was the work of Dostoevsky, a socialist sympathizer transformed by the experience of mock execution and incarceration in a labour camp into an Orthodox believer, a conservative, and by far the greatest 'theological' writer of the nineteenth century. The memoirs, novels, and stories that Dostoevsky wrote after his return from Siberian exile were not 'religious' merely in the sense that they focused upon themes of transgression and repentance, or topical issues such as the reform of the church courts, or because they included characters who were believers. They were also permeated by religious concepts that shaped structure and plot as well as appearing in arguments, most importantly *sobornost* (a term coined by Khomyakov to describe a social unity modelled upon that of the *sobornaya tserkov*, the phrase used for 'Holy Catholic Church' in the Orthodox Creed) and *kenosis* ('emptying out', a term denominating the striving to commune with others, to the point of self-loss). Both of these concepts were central to Dostoevsky's final and most obviously Orthodox novel, *The Brothers Karamazov* (1879–80). They underlay the portraits of Alyosha Karamazov and of his teacher Zosima, whose godly death was a counterbalance to the brutal parricide at the heart of the novel. They were also at the heart of the Fable of the Grand Inquisitor, where the Inquisitor himself spoke for a utilitarian, 'Western' view of Church power working in the world to right material injustice, while the silent Christ stood for spiritual probity of a non-interventionist, contemplative kind.

At some levels, then, there could scarcely be a more instructive contrast in styles than between Pushkin and Dostoevsky. On the one hand, there is *The Brothers Karamazov*, a sprawling, immensely ambitious study of the nature of belief, if also of the nature of doubt (there is passionate conviction in the agnostic Ivan Karamazov's refusal to acknowledge the goodness of a deity who tolerates suffering on the part of the innocent). On the other, there is *The Queen of Spades*, a brilliant miniature in which the existence even of the supernatural in a low-level sense, let alone of God, is open to question, and in which the Church figures only in the form of a worldly priest whose lip-service to the moral qualities of the dead Countess in his funeral oration is in ironic contrast to her querulous and egotistical character in life. Dostoevsky's admiration for Pushkin (even a Pushkin made in his own image) seems at first mysterious. Yet the two tales do have much in common, and not just because Pushkin's frivolous *beau-monde* is the world in which Elder Zosima has moved before his conversion. Similar, too, is the matter-of-fact, even homely, attitude to the uncanny in both texts. The dead Countess's appearance to Hermann in *The Queen of Spades* (whether as hallucination or ghost is unclear) is preceded by 'a shuffling of slippers'; the Devil who appears to Ivan in *The Brothers Karamazov* is a disagreeably chirpy middle-aged man whose mediocre brown suit suggests a middle-ranking provincial civil servant, the Evil One as pen-pushing bureaucrat.

The other world as seen here is, in the words of Svidrigailov, Raskolnikov's sinister double in *Crime and Punishment*, hell as 'a bath-house full of spiders'. The chilling sense of a sort of parallel universe of banality and boredom recurs in Daniil Kharms' absurdist stories of the 1930s, here acting as a counterweight to the synthetic 'heaven' of Socialist Realist myth. It is present once more in the figure of Quilty from *Lolita*, a travesty Doppelgänger whom Humbert Humbert cannot throw off, any more than Ivan can his horribly bonhomous devil. In all these texts, the sense of hellish claustrophobia retains its hold, but in each it is modulated quite differently. It never hardens into stereotype, unlike the view of everyday life as a domain of inescapable banality, an impediment to intellectual activity, which gives many Russian texts, from Chernyshevsky's *What is to Be Done* to the final part of Pasternak's *Doctor Zhivago*, a strange vacancy at their heart, with specific settings treated as though they were of no more consequence than the standard fittings of a station waiting room before a train is boarded to head off somewhere more interesting. The most vivid evocations of Christ in Russian literature are of failed Christs: Prince Myshkin in *The Idiot*, whose commitment to salvation through love destroys Nastas'ya Filippovna rather than saving her, and Ieshua, the eccentric, holy-fool Jesus of Bulgakov's debunked Jerusalem in *Master and Margarita*.

If the canonical Gospel texts have been reflected in Russian literature only obliquely, though, the absorption of writers in eschatology, or the 'four last things' of Christian theology (death, judgement, heaven, and hell), has made the Apocalypse a central book for them. This is particularly clear in texts written during the late nineteenth and early twentieth centuries. The pessimism of the *fin de siècle* inspired interest not only in the writings of such intellectual nihilists as Nietzsche or Oswald Spengler, but also in the Orthodox tradition of looking forward to the destruction of the wicked secular world and the establishment of religious rule. Successive historical catastrophes – national defeat in the Russo-Japanese War in 1905 and the 'year of revolutions' that followed, the First World War, Revolution, and the Russian Civil War – were represented by writers using apocalyptic imagery. A particularly striking example was Bulgakov's novel *The White Guard*. The book had some allegiance to the historical fiction of Tolstoy, in that the experience of one family and their connections was used to stand for the experience of historical subjects in general. But Tolstoy's emphasis upon history as a dialectic between predestination and human will (according to the epilogue of *War and Peace*, the wise historical subject was one who did not place too high a value upon the import of his or her own actions) had been replaced by a stress on malign destiny. This reinforced the powerlessness of historical subjects, who were left only with the power to regret. In this, Bulgakov echoed the moralism of Russian medieval texts such as *The Tale of the Destruction of Ryazan by Baty*, where defeat and destruction were visited upon God's people 'because of our sins': 'A great year but a fearful year was the year of Our Lord 1918', the novel begins, and the arrival in Kiev of the vicious peasant leader Petlyura, tales of whose atrocities are shown spreading round the city as he approaches, is accompanied by cosmic portents:

> Quite suddenly the grey background in the gap between the domes burst open, and an unexpected sun showed in swirling dark dimness. It was vaster than any sun people in the Ukraine had ever seen, and a true scarlet, like pure blood.

> (Chapter 16)

In a world where the immanence if not the existence of God had become subject to serious doubt, it was the antichrist, and satanic forces more generally, that could be imagined as physically present in the material world. Just so, when the body – notably absent from Romantic and Symbolist writing – re-asserted itself in the writing of Russian Modernism, this was often as a detested 'envelope' for the mind or the spirit. The hatred felt by the narrators of Yury Olesha's *Envy*, or Nabokov's *Lolita*, for their physical selves is matched in Joseph Brodsky's poem 'The Year 1972', which represents the lyric hero's self as 'stinking of breath and creaking of joints/a blot on the mirror' and with 'enough caries in my teeth/to map out Ancient Greece, at least'.

The emphasis on death and punishment has often drawn (usually implicitly rather than explicitly) on the strong vein of anti-physicality in Russian Orthodox culture. Earlier manifestations of this in Russian literature had included Derzhavin's 'On the Death of Prince Meshchersky' (1779), which stressed the universality of decay ('The monarch and the captive are alike food for worms'). Later ones included Tolstoy's *Confession* (1879–80), with its extraordinary image, borrowed from an Eastern legend, of the living human suspended over the abyss on a tree-trunk gnawed by a serpent. But if Derzhavin's or Tolstoy's response to the inevitability of death had been to stress the importance of a virtuous life, twentieth-century texts tended to represent the alternative and better reality as something elusive and insubstantial. It was associated with mysterious, uncommunicable experience, what Aleksandr Blok called, in one of his poems addressed to the Beautiful Lady, 'the call of dim life/Splashing secretly within me'. It manifested itself in the colours of 'non-being', of death and of spiritual life at one and the same time, whiteness and transparency. Though, as David Bethea has pointed out, Utopian writing was the polar opposite of apocalyptic writing, in that it anticipated a paradise in the future (often a technological one) rather than mourning the loss of the 'original pristine faith' of the past, in practice the two discourses often exploited similar imagery – as, indeed, did Socialist Realism, whose spotless factories, ever-patient party officials, and peaceful, hard-working labourers made it a form of bastardized Utopianism. Just so did the traditions of pre-Petrine Russian religious literature find themselves preserved in Socialist Realism's earnest commitment to expressing the 'elevated belief of human beings in Sublimity', as a typical Soviet Realist, Vera Panova, put it in 1972.

But not all Russian literature by any means has been driven by a puritanical distaste for quotidian existence, for the material world. Some writers (the early twentieth-century short-story writer Aleksey Remizov, for instance) gave their demons the comforting substance of folk myth, of the malevolent creatures (house spirits and wood demons) that had to be placated with bread and milk. Mandelstam rebelled against the Symbolist emphasis upon esoteric myth by proclaiming the virtues of 'domestic Hellenism', of ordinary, though handsome, objects such as jugs and honey-jars. Other writers created a kind of 'domestic Orthodoxy', of mundane but fervent spirituality. Olga Sedakova's limpid poem 'Old Women', for example, sees the secular and the spiritual, the sinful and the pious, as inseparably fused:

> Patient as an Old Master,
> I love to study the faces
> of pious, spiteful old women,

the mortality of their lips,

and the immortality of the power

that pressed their lips together,

(like an angel squatting

and stacking coppers in piles,

five copecks, and light copeck pieces . . .

'Shoo!' he says to the children,

the birds and the beggars,

'Shoo, go away,' he tells them:

can't you see what I'm doing?) –

I stare, and in my mind I sketch them,

like my own face, in a glass darkly.

The images of a money-counting angel and of 'spiteful piety' are contradictory and even shocking. They recall Rembrandt's late portraits of elderly women (hence the phrase 'Patient as an Old Master'), in which supreme artistic beauty is made out of material that is not obviously handsome (unlike the jugs and jars celebrated by Mandelstam). In the same way, the nineteenth-century prose writer Nikolay Leskov's stories turned the early nineteenth-century Russian provinces into an extraordinary retrospective Utopia, a world of small-mindedness and prejudice against outsiders, but also of sanity, tolerance, and bodily joy. His extraordinary and touching tale, The Sealed Angel (1873), expressed a vision of art as at once profoundly spiritual and rooted in reality: a combination of inspiration in its most literal sense and of careful craftsmanship. The icon of the title is not only a symbol of faith repressed by bureaucracy (it is confiscated and 'sealed' with a layer of wax, in a sublime gesture of secular indifference to the uniqueness of the icon), but also of religious art. As explained by the Red-Haired Man, the story's main narrator, and a member of the conservative and pious Old Believer sect, to a well-intentioned but sceptical Englishman, the icon stands for a kind of artistic integrity to be found only in traditional practices:

The Englishman did not believe me, so I went and explained the whole difference to him: nowadays, I said, worldly artists didn't make the same kind of art; they used paints made of oil, while the old artists, they used pigments dissolved in egg-yolk. The new art, that means you smear the paint on so it only looks life-like in the distance, while in the old kind the work is smooth, and even close to, you can see it clearly. And a worldly artist, I said, won't even get things right in the outline of his drawing, because he's been taught to represent what's hidden in the body of the earthly and animal man, but in holy Russian icon-painting is represented the face that dwelleth in heaven, which a material person could never see even in his imagination.

Yet this other-worldly art, as the detailed description here makes clear, is also one of exact representation. As evoked by the Red-Haired Man, the angel icon at the centre of the story has an individual and distinct physical presence. His face is not only 'radiant divine' (*svetlobozhestvennyi*) but also 'kind of ready to help' (*edak skoropomoshchnyi*).

'Domestic Orthodoxy', then, consists not in a rejection of the material world, but in the notion of a fusion of the material and the spiritual as the ideal. In this it has something in common with another salutary response to the clichés of other-worldliness, the construction of a theology of the body. The origins of this can be traced back to some writers associated with the national-conservative Slavophile movement. In Tolstoy's eulogies of procreative family life in *War and Peace* and *Anna Karenina*, the rare moments of perfect happiness are associated with a celebration of physical intimacy – Natasha waving her baby's nappies in front of friends, or (more decorously) Lyovin watching Kitty bathe his son. To be sure, Tolstoy's energetic love of the physical was determinedly anti-sexual: it is child-bearing rather than copulation that is a source of true joy (the fact that Lyovin and Kitty find sexual contact embarrassing but child-rearing unambiguously enjoyable makes this perfectly clear). But a later Slavophile writer, the brilliant essayist Vasily

20. 'Don't Weep for Me, Mother': The Saviour not Made by Human Hands with Saints. Icon for Holy Week: a Muscovite version of the Greek *acheiropoietos*, as evoked in the first line of 'Monument', showing the triumph of the resurrected Christ over the tomb.

Rozanov, created a world where there was no separation between body and spirit, flesh and intellect. As the scholar Stephen Hutchings has pointed out, Rozanov's was an existence where 'the most exaggeratedly profound formulations are arrived at "over a cup of tea" or "in the lavatory"'. The writer firmly believed that 'a hole in a sock that never grows larger, and never gets darned' was a better expression of everlasting life than 'the dry and abstract term "immortality of the soul"', and believed sexuality was an essential, indeed perhaps the essential, form of spiritual expression. In his *People of the Lunar Light*, Rozanov insisted upon the perverted nature of religious celibacy (monasticism was for him a form of displaced, or not so displaced, homo-eroticism); procreative sexuality, preferably ritualized in the way that it was by Jews (who reserved copulation for the eve of the Sabbath) was a godly act. Sexuality, too, was the only way of resolving the otherwise unresolvable problem of how to produce a dialogue between self and other, retaining the identity of each yet allowing free communication between them.

A similar attempt to embrace the bodily world is evident in one of the most enlivening and vivid responses to Socialist Realism, Mikhail Bakhtin's study of François Rabelais, which celebrated the physicality of the 'carnival', glorifying the temporary suspension of rational decorum and the resurgence of 'the lower bodily stratum'. Bakhtin's concept of the carnival drew on a great deal more than the actual practices of fairgrounds and folk festivals, though the fashion for circus and vaudeville in 1920s Soviet literature, theatre, and film was definitely part of the background to the book. Rather, the evocation of the medieval carnival was used to create an imaginative space with many kinds of cultural resonance. Among these are the Stalin regime's own promotion of a decorous and conformist kind of carnival, the Symbolists' fascination with Dionysiac religion, in which the body of the god was repeatedly destroyed and repeatedly made whole, and popular traditions about lands of plenty and joy beyond the known world (as evoked also in Aleksandr Chayanov's *Journey of My Brother Aleksei to the*

Land of Peasant Utopia, written in 1920). But Bakhtin's book was also related to the writings of Khomyakov, Ivan Kireevsky, and Konstantin Aksakov in its emphasis upon community ritual, and in its sense of religious experience in the everyday. The various elements can be seen coming together, for instance, in his description of the banquet.

> In the act of eating, as we have said, the confines between the body and the world are overstepped by the body. It triumphs over the world, over its enemy, celebrates its victory, grows at the world's expense. This element of victory and triumph is inherent in all banquet images. No meal can be sad. Sadness and food are incompatible (while death and food are perfectly compatible). The banquet always celebrates a victory and this is part of its very nature. Further, the triumphant banquet is always universal. It is the triumph of life over death. In this respect it is equivalent to conception and birth. The victorious body receives the defeated world and is renewed.
>
> (Chapter 4)

Popular feasting and the Christian Eucharist, with its link to resurrection on the one hand and crucifixion on the other, come together in a tour-de-force of neo-Slavophile cultural criticism, which synthesizes rather than analyses and is rooted in a determination to celebrate the wholeness of life, and not to discriminate between 'aesthetic' and 'anti-aesthetic', acceptable and unacceptable, sensations.

Bakhtin's book is also a tribute to the vitality of humour in Russian culture, as, too, are Rozanov's miniatures, not only the vessels of 'exaggerated profundity' but of studiedly ridiculous self-portraits – having confiscated his children's Sherlock Holmes stories as 'harmful reading', Rozanov devoured them himself at every possible opportunity, 'so that the train journey from Siverskaya to St Petersburg flew past like a dream'. A popular Western view of Russia sees the place as grim, dank, and with permanently gloomy inhabitants given to fits of weeping and talking about their souls. No one could maintain this illusion for long when reading Russian literature. In Chekhov's plays, even characters prone to maudlin fits of self-pity display a talent for flights of black comedy (as when Uncle Vanya responds to a social banality about the nice weather with the words, 'Nice weather to hang yourself in'). Here, humour is a weapon for exposing artificiality (as it also is in Dostoevsky's novels, where lapses into absurdity threaten every carefully planned social event). But ridicule is often more universal than this, giving a sense of human existence as necessarily grotesque – as in the scene from Chekhov's 'Ward No. 6' (1892) where one madman boasts of his fantasy service decorations to another invalided out of the civil service when he became wrongly convinced he was making mistakes and developed paranoia.

Black humour of this kind survived at even the darkest eras of history, such as the late 1930s. To be sure, in Socialist Realist texts, humour that was not of the unintentional sort was limited to crude jokes directed at a narrow range of social types (shirkers at work, women who used too much make-up, men who tried to lay down the law to their wives). In unofficial writing, though, a vivid and subtle feeling of the ridiculous survived, and pompous bureaucrats were its main targets (in Bulgakov's *Master and Margarita*, comic vengeance is exacted on a whole crowd of such people). In texts of this kind, humour was a survival strategy, but it was also a manifestation of freedom, a means of transcending oppression, a gesture of indifference towards authority. The exhilirating carnival foolery celebrated by Bakhtin was only one form of challenging official puritanism. The humour of the 'holy fools', the popular saints of early modern Russia whose filthy habits and bizarre behaviour assailed ordinary proprieties, and thus called into question conventional ideas about goodness, also worked its way through into some later literary texts. Kostoglotov, the protagonist of Solzhenitsyn's *Cancer Ward*, who is saddled with an absurd name (Boneswallower), and is, in every obvious way, decidedly unamiable – surly, brusque, unrepentantly naive – moved like some latterday, secularized version of the holy fool through 1950s Soviet society, saving no one but himself, yet at the same time exposing the illusions upon which the ideals and aspirations of those surrounding him were based.

The uniqueness of Russian literature (and Russian culture more generally) has been held by many Western observers to lie in precisely this ability to embrace spiritual and material worlds. As the classicist and Russophile Jane Harrison declared in 1919, 'The Russian stands for the complexity and concreteness of life – felt whole, unanalysed, unjudged, lived into . . .'. But as I come to the end of this short tour along pathways suggested by Pushkin's 'Monument', I would not want to leave you with the impression that this chapter has spoken 'the last word', that we have reached the heart of the maze. Rather, there is no such heart: we have met the beginning of a path leading backward. For Pushkin, the last word was not 'O Muse, be obedient to the command of God', but 'Don't dispute with fools': which leads back to the discussion of *savoir faire* placed here in Chapter 6. We saw in Chapter 5 that *judging* life has been a constant preoccupation of Russian writers, while Pushkin himself is an illustration that intelligent Russians have had just as large a talent for, and inclination towards, *analysis* as their counterparts anywhere in the world. In Russia itself, writers have often been regarded as sages, as moral guides to how life should be lived; but there are many other reasons for reading Russian literature. Like any other literature, it represents the world in new and extraordinary ways, it investigates areas of human experience that we sometimes prefer not to think about (madness, homicidal urges, tyranny); and it offers not only intellectual stimulation but the sensual delight of language stretched to its limits, of laughter, and of flights of imaginative fancy.

Further reading

Preface

N. Cornwell (ed.), *A Reference Guide to Russian Literature* (London, 1998), and V. Terras (ed.), *Handbook of Russian Literature* (New Haven, Conn., 1984) (the latter lists more writers, but the bibliographies and articles in the former are fuller). Among single-volume histories are R. Hingley, *Russian Writers and Society* (London, 1975) and *Russian Writers and Soviet Society* (London, 1978); D. S. Mirsky, *History of Russian Literature* (New York, 1949); C. Moser (ed.), *The Cambridge History of Russian Literature* (Cambridge, 1992); V. Terras, *A History of Russian Literature* (New Haven, Conn., 1991); R. Bartlett and A. Benn (eds.), *Literary Russia: A Guide* (London, 1997) is useful on museums. Fuller reading lists, as well as source notes for the entire book, are available on the OUP website at //http.www.oup.com/

Chapter 1

The *Complete Pushkin in English* began publication in 1999. Recent single-volume translations include *Pushkin's Notebooks in Facsimile* (London, 1995-8); A. D. P. Briggs (ed.), *Alexander Pushkin: Selections* (London, 1997); E. Feinstein (ed.), *Pushkin Translated* (Manchester, 1999); A. Kahn (ed.), *Tales of the Late Ivan Petrovich Belkin, The Queen of Spades, The Captain's Daughter, Peter the Great's Blackamoor* (Oxford, 1997). See also 'A Pushkin Portfolio', *Modern Poetry in Translation* 15 (1999), 144-277; *Eugene Onegin, Translated with a Commentary by Vladimir*

Nabokov (Princeton, NJ, 1981); T. Shaw (ed.), *The Letters of Alexander Pushkin* (Bloomington, Ind., 1963).

Chapter 2

D. Bethea, *Realizing Metaphors: Alexander Pushkin and the Life of the Poet* (Madison, Wisconsin, 1998); P. Debreczeny, 'Zhitie Aleksandra Boldinskogo: Pushkin's Elevation to Sainthood in Soviet Culture', *South Atlantic Quarterly* 90 (1991), 269–302; M. C. Levitt, *Russian Literary Politics and the Pushkin Celebration of 1880* (Ithaca, NY, 1989); K. Petrone, *Life Has Become Joyous, Comrades: Celebrations in the Time of Stalin* (Bloomington, Ind., 2000), chapter 5; A. Siniavsky, *Strolls with Pushkin* (New Haven, Conn., 1993); S. Vitale, *Pushkin's Button* (London, 1999). See also the chapters by M. C. Levitt and S. Sandler in B. Gasparov, R. C. Hughes, and I. Paperno (eds.), *Cultural Mythologies of Russian Modernism: From the Golden Age to the Silver Age* (Berkeley, 1992).

Chapter 3

For Pushkin's own views on the canon, see Tatiana Woolf (ed.), *Pushkin on Literature* (London, 1971). C. R. S. Cockrell and D. Richards (eds.), *Russian Views of Pushkin* (Oxford, 1976) and S. Hoisington (ed.), *Russian Views of Pushkin's Evgeny Onegin* (Bloomington, Ind., 1988) are useful anthologies of critical opinion. More generally, see J. Brooks, 'Russian Nationalism and Russian Literature: The Canonization of the Classics', in I. Banac, J. G. Ackerman, and R. Szporluk (eds.), *Nation and Ideology* (1981), 315–34; M. Friedberg, *Russian Classics in Soviet Jackets* (New York, 1962); S. Lovell, *The Russian Reading Revolution: Print Culture in the Soviet and Post-Soviet Eras* (Basingstoke, 2000). On censorship, see M. T. Choldin and M. Friedberg (eds.), *The Red Pencil: Artists, Scholars, and Censors in the USSR* (Boston, 1989); M. Dewhirst and R. Farrell (eds.), *The Soviet Censorship* (Metuchen, NJ, 1973); D. Jones (ed.), *Literary Censorship: A Reference Guide* (London, 2001); L. Losev, *On the Beneficence of Censorship: Aesopian Language in Modern Russian Literature* (Munich, 1984).

Chapter 4

L. Ginzburg, *On Psychological Prose* (Princeton, NJ, 1990); G. S. Morson, *Hidden in Plain View: Narrative and Creative Potentials in War and Peace* (Berkeley, 1987); A. Wachtel, *An Obsession with History: Russian Writers Confront the Past* (Stanford, 1994).

Chapter 5

For nineteenth-century Russian literature and politics, see Isaiah Berlin, *Russian Thinkers* (London, 1978); Aileen Kelly, *Toward Another Shore: Russian Thinkers between Necessity and Chance* (New Haven, 1998) and her *Views from the Other Shore: Essays on Herzen, Chekhov, and Bakhtin* (New Haven, 1999); Leonard Schapiro, *Turgenev: His Life and Times* (Oxford, 1978). On the twentieth century, see K. Clark, *The Soviet Novel: History as Ritual* (Chicago, 1981); G. Freidin, *A Coat of Many Colors: Osip Mandelstam and his Mythologies of Self-Preservation* (Berkeley, 1987); J. Garrard and C. Garrard, *Inside the Soviet Writers' Union* (London, 1990); T. Lahusen, *How Life Writes the Book: Real Socialism and Socialist Realism in Stalin's Russia* (Ithaca, NY, 1997); R. Robin, *Socialist Realism: An Impossible Aesthetic* (Stanford, 1992); D. Shepherd, *Beyond Metafiction: Self-Consciousness in Soviet Literature* (Oxford, 1992); G. S. Smith, *D. S. Mirsky: A Russian-English Life* (Oxford, 2000), part 3.

Chapter 6

J. Andrew (ed.), *Russian Women's Shorter Fiction: An Anthology 1835–1860* (Oxford, 1996); H. Goscilo and B. Holmgren (eds.), *Russia – Women – Culture* (Bloomington, Ind., 1997); B. Heldt, *Terrible Perfection: Women in Russian Literature* (Bloomington, Ind., 1987); B. Holmgren, *Women's Work in Stalin's Times* (Bloomington, Ind., 1993); C. Kelly (ed.), *An Anthology of Russian Women's Writing, 1777–1992* (Oxford, 1994) and C. Kelly, *A History of Russian Women's Writing, 1820–1992* (Oxford, 1994); M. Ledkovsky, C. Rosenthal, and M. Zirin (eds.), *A Dictionary of Russian Women Writers* (Westport, Conn., 1994); L. Ya. Ginzburg, Yu. M. Lotman, and B. Uspensky, *The Semiotics of Russian Cultural History* (Ithaca, NY, 1985); I. Reyfman, *Ritualized Violence Russian Style: The Duel in Russian*

Culture and Literature (Stanford, 1999); W. M. Todd III, *Fiction and Society in the Age of Pushkin: Ideology, Institutions, and Narrative* (Cambridge, Mass., 1986).

Chapter 7

J. Andrew, *Narrative and Desire in Russian Literature: The Feminine and The Masculine* (Basingstoke, 1993); M. Makin, *Marina Tsvetaeva: The Poetics of Appropriation* (Oxford, 1994), chapter 3; F. J. Oinas, *Essays in Russian Folklore and Mythology* (Columbus, Ohio, 1975); D. E. Peterson, *Up From Bondage: The Literature of Russian and African-American Soul* (Durham, NC, 2000); S. Sandler, *Distant Pleasures: Aleksandr Pushkin and the Writing of Exile* (Stanford, 1989); J. West in R. Anderson and Paul Debreczeny, *Russian Narrative and Visual Art: Varieties of Seeing* (Gainesville, Florida, 1994).

Chapter 8

S. Baehr, *The Paradise Myth in Eighteenth-Century Russia* (Stanford, 1991); J. Billington, *The Icon and the Axe* (London, 1966); C. Brandist, *Carnival Culture in the Soviet Modernist Novel* (Basingstoke, 1996); P. Davidson (ed.), *Russian Literature and its Demons* (London, 2000); S. Hutchings, *Russian Modernism: The Transfiguration of the Everyday* (Cambridge, 1997); E. Naiman, *Sex in Public: The Incarnation of Early Soviet Literature* (Ithaca, NY, 1997); R. Stites, *Revolutionary Dreams: Utopian Visions and Experimental Life in the Russian Revolution* (Oxford, 1989).

Index

References in **bold type** are to explanatory text-boxes.

A

Aeschylus 9

Akhmatova, Anna
(1889–1966), poet 5, 18, 24,
26–7, 73, 88, 91, 103, 109, 111,
112–13, 115

Alexander I (reigned 1801–25),
Emperor of Russia 13

Aksakov, Konstantin (1817–60),
Slavophile thinker 150

Aleshkovsky, Yuz (b. 1929),
novelist 136

Amfiteatrov, Aleksandr
(1862–1938), prose writer
93

Annenkov, Pavel (1812 or
1813–87), critic 77

Annensky, Innokenty (1855 or
1856–1909), poet 62

Antokolsky, Pavel (1896–1978),
poet 91

Apollo (literary journal) 37–8, 42

Austen, Jane 43, 102

B

Bakhtin, Mikhail (1895–1975),
cultural critic 85, 149

Baratynsky, Evgeny (1800–44),
poet 110, 140

Barrett, Thomas 122

Batyushkov, Konstantin
(1787–1855), poet 110

Beckett, Samuel 133

Belinsky, Vissarion
(1811–48), critic 39, 41, 47,
76, 81, 139

Bely, Andrey (1880–1934),
novelist and poet 16, 62

Bethea, David 145

Bishop, Elizabeth 28

Blake, William 43

Blok, Aleksandr (1881–1921), poet
59, 111, 126, 128, 145

Boborykin, Petr (1836–1921),
prose writer 93

body, theology of 149

Bowen, Elizabeth 6

Boym, Svetlana (b. 1959), critic
92

Brik, Osip (1888–1945), critic
139

Brodsky, Joseph (1940–96),
poet v, 5, 8, 71–3, 91, 144

Brontë, Emily 43

Bryusov, Valery (1874–1924),
poet 82, 132

Buchan, John 120

Buck, Pearl S. 5

Bulgakov, Mikhail (1891–1940),
novelist and dramatist 29,
89, 143–4

Bulgarin, Faddey (1789–1859),
novelist, journalist, and spy
80

Bunina, Anna (1774–1829), poet
114

Russian Literature

Index